100 Classic
Gluten-Free
Comfort Food
Recipes

Donna Washburn & Heather Butt

Robert
ROSE

For complete cataloguing information, see page 224.

Disclaimer
The recipes in this book have been carefully tested by our kitchen and our tasters. To the best of our knowledge, they are safe and nutritious for ordinary use and users. For those people with food or other allergies, or who have special food requirements or health issues, please read the suggested contents of each recipe carefully and determine whether or not they may create a problem for you. All recipes are used at the risk of the consumer.

When using specialized appliances, consumers should always consult their manufacturer's manual for recommended procedures and cooking times. We cannot be responsible for any hazards, loss or damage that may occur as a result of any recipe use.

For those with special needs, allergies, requirements or health problems, in the event of any doubt, please contact your medical adviser prior to the use of any recipe.

Design and production: Daniella Zanchetta/PageWave Graphics Inc.
Editor: Meredith Dees
Recipe editor: Jennifer MacKenzie
Proofreader: Linda Pruessen
Indexer: Gillian Watts

Cover image: Strawberry Shortcake (page 128)
Back cover images: Vegetarian Pizza (page 50), Fudgy Brownies (page 154), Oven-Fried Chicken (page 70)

Photography Credits:
Cover and interior photos/prop styling by Jan Kalish; food styling/prop styling by Chantal Payette, *except as noted below*. Photographs copyright © 2017 Jan Kalish.

Photos on pages 39, 47, 71, 107, 111, 125, 133, 138, 153, 161, 167, 201 and 207 by Colin Ericson; food styling by Kate Bush/Kathryn Robertson; prop styling by Charlene Ericson. Photographs copyright © 2017 Robert Rose Inc.

Photos on pages 42 and 187 by Matt Johannsson; food styling by Michael Elliott; prop styling by Charlene Ericson. Photographs copyright © 2017 Robert Rose Inc.

The publisher gratefully acknowledges the financial support of our publishing program by the Government of Canada through the Canada Book Fund.

Canadä

Published by Robert Rose Inc.
120 Eglinton Avenue East, Suite 800, Toronto, Ontario, Canada M4P 1E2
Tel: (416) 322-6552 Fax: (416) 322-6936
www.robertrose.ca

Printed and bound in Canada

1 2 3 4 5 6 7 8 9 TCP 25 24 23 22 21 20 19 18 17

We dedicate this book to everyone who has encouraged us over the years. Your support and friendship mean a lot to us. We wish we had room to list all your names.

Chocolate Chip Cookies (page 147)

Contents

Acknowledgments 6

Introduction. 7

Understanding Whole Grains 8

Other Gluten-Free Baking Ingredients 13

Nutrient Content of Gluten-Free Grains, Flours
    and Starches 20

Using an Instant-Read Thermometer 22

Speaking Our Language:
    Are We All on the Same Page? 25

Soups and Salads 27

Entrées and Sides 43

Yeast Breads 93

Yeast-Free Muffins and Biscuits 117

Cookies, Bars and Squares 139

Cakes. 157

Pies and Pastry 177

Puddings and Other Sweets 193

Equipment Glossary 209

Ingredient Glossary. 211

Techniques Glossary 216

About the Nutrient Analysis 219

Index 220

Acknowledgments

This book has had the support and assistance of many, from its inception to the final version. We want to thank those who helped us along the way.

Our thanks to the following people and companies for supplying products for recipe development: George Birinyi Jr. of Grain Process Enterprises Ltd. for potato starch, tapioca starch, sorghum flour, amaranth flour, almond meal and xanthan gum; Howard Selig of Valley Flaxflour Ltd. for flax flour and flax seeds, both brown and golden; Doug Yuen of Dainty Foods for brown rice flour and rice bran; Margaret Hughes of Best Cooking Pulses, Inc. for BEST Whole Yellow Pea Flour and Chickpea Flour; Michel Dion of Lallemand Inc. for Eagle Instaferm® yeast; Beth Armour and Tracy Perry of Cream Hill Estates for oat flour and rolled oats; Tilley Wiens of Avena Foods Ltd. for Only Oats, oat bran, oat flour, steel-cut oats and rolled oats; Northern Quinoa Corp. for NorQuin Brand golden quinoa flour and Canadian-grown Norquin Brand quinoa; Richardson Oilseed, Richardson International Ltd. for Canola Harvest canola oil; Workinesh Spice Blends, Inc. for teff flour; and Margaret Hudson of Burnbrae Farms Ltd. for Naturegg Simply Egg Whites and Break-Free liquid eggs.

Thank you to the many manufacturers of bread machines, who continue to supply our test kitchen with the latest models: Zojirushi, Cuisinart, Spectrum Brands Breadman® and Hamilton Beach Brands.

A huge thank you to the members of our focus group, who faithfully and tirelessly tasted and tested gluten-free recipes and products from the beginning to the end of our recipe development. Your comments, suggestions and critical analysis were invaluable and helped make this a better book.

We want to express our appreciation to photographers Jan Kalish, Colin Erricson and Matt Johannsson, food stylists Chantal Payette, Kathryn Robertson, Michael Elliot and Kate Bush, and prop stylists Jan Kalish, Chantal Payette and Charlene Erricson. Thank you for making our gluten-free foods look delicious.

Bob Dees, our publisher; Marian Jarkovich, Director, Sales and Marketing; Martine Quibell, Manager, Publicity; and Nina McCreath, Manager, Corporate Accounts and International Sales at Robert Rose Inc., deserve special thanks for their ongoing support. Thanks to our new editor, Meredith Dees. We enjoyed working with you.

A very special thanks to Magda Fahmy-Turnbull, RD, for her work on the nutritional analysis. She has been an invaluable resource throughout this project.

Thank you to our families and friends: you helped bring balance to our lives when we became too focused on our work.

And finally, to you who must follow a gluten-free diet: we sincerely hope these recipes help make your life easier and more enjoyable. We developed them with you in mind.

— *Donna and Heather*

Introduction

It is a beautiful autumn day today. The maple trees are more brilliantly red and orange than they have been for several years. The sun is shining, and we should be outside in our gardens, but instead we are busy in the test kitchen.

When we were asked to develop recipes for this new cookbook of gluten-free classics, we immediately accepted. Not only did it allow us to work together again — best friends for 36 years — but research for this book allowed us to take a journey into our past. First, we brainstormed. Then we scoured our mothers' and grandmothers' cookbooks and asked friends. Finally, we scrolled through the Internet. We wanted to create a collection of recipes that reminded us of the favorites we grew up with and still enjoy today.

Each recipe brought back a childhood memory of a special meal, a holiday or a school lunch. We spent hours just chatting about these events! So much of our lives revolve around food, and reliving these experiences and choosing the recipes was fun for us. We made sure that only the best were included, and we hope each of them will evoke a special memory for you, too.

Our introduction wouldn't be complete without a mention of nutrition, which has always been important to us. Although these recipes are classics, they contain lower sodium, sugar and fat than the favorites you know and love, while maintaining the flavor you have come to expect from us. We bake with nutritious flours, choosing only those that result in great taste and textures you will enjoy. Every recipe is accompanied by a nutritional analysis. You'll find extra information about each flour, and how to store and use individual ingredients, on pages 9–12, giving you the information you need to make healthy decisions for you and your family.

As we developed these recipes, we kept in mind your busy lifestyle today. We have shortened methods, added relevant tips to each and, once again, included three glossaries.

We wish we could be in your homes as you prepare these recipes for your families. We are sure they will evoke happy memories for you, too.

Donna Washburn and Heather Butt
Quality Professional Services
1655 County Rd. #2
Mallorytown, ON
K0E 1R0
bestbreadrecipes@gmail.com
Website: www.bestbreadrecipes.com
Facebook: @bestbreadrecipesbooks

Understanding Whole Grains

"A whole grain is the entire seed, including the naturally occurring nutrients of an edible plant. The size, shape and color of the seed, also referred to as the 'kernel,' vary with the species."

— Oldways Whole Grains Council

A grain consists of three parts: the bran, the germ and the endosperm. The **bran**, or outer coating, is made up of several layers. It is rich in insoluble fiber and contains antioxidants and B vitamins. Just beneath the bran layers is a small structure called the **germ**. The germ is rich in healthy oils, B vitamins, minerals, including magnesium and iron, and some protein. The **endosperm** is the largest portion of the grain. It contains starch, protein, soluble fiber and small amounts of vitamins and minerals.

Whole grains contain all three parts, whereas refined grains (white rice, defatted soy, degerminated cornmeal) have the bran and germ removed, leaving only the endosperm. Refined grains are not as nutritious as whole grains. Some refined grains may be enriched (some of the nutrients that were removed are added back), but few gluten-free (GF) grains, flours or products are enriched. It is very important to read labels every time when purchasing products made commercially with GF flours.

Whole grains can be eaten whole, cracked, ground or milled into flour. A whole grain that has been processed (cracked, crushed, ground, milled, rolled, extruded and/or cooked) still contains approximately the same nutrients found in the original grain seed.

Flour is the ground form of a grain. It can be milled from the whole grain or may be a refined and processed grain. Many gluten-free flours are whole grains.

Whole Grain Anatomy

Source: Oldways Whole Grains Council. (Used with permission.) **www.wholegrainscouncil.org**

GF Whole Grains

- amaranth
- buckwheat
- corn, including whole cornmeal
- GF oats, including oatmeal
- millet
- quinoa
- rice, both brown and colored
- sorghum
- teff
- wild rice

(Approved and endorsed by the Oldways Whole Grains Council, May 2004)

Gluten-Free Whole Grains

Amaranth flour is fine-textured, with a light cream color and a pleasant, nutty taste. Because of its high moisture content, we recommend using it in combination with other flours. It produces baked goods that are moist and dense, but the added starch helps to lighten the texture. The grain of the bread is more open, the texture not as silky and the crumb color slightly darker than wheat flour products. Amaranth flour tends to form a crust on the outside of a product during baking, sealing the outside before the product is completely cooked on the inside, so use the smallest amount of liquid you can and allow for slightly longer baking times than you might otherwise. Products baked with amaranth flour tend to brown quickly and may need to be tented with foil during the last third of the baking time. Check to make sure the internal temperature of the baked product reaches 200°F (100°C) — it may look baked on the outside before the center is done. We enjoy amaranth flour in yeast breads, muffins, cookies, pancakes and flatbreads. It is one of our favorites for thickening gravy, soups and stews because it results in a dull finish and holds well (see Roux, Techniques Glossary, page 218).

Buckwheat is available as groats, kasha (roasted, toasted groats), flakes and flour. **Buckwheat flour** is very fine, with a unique, strong, musty, slightly sour, slightly nutty flavor. For light buckwheat flour, the hull is removed before the groats are ground. Dark buckwheat flour is made of unhulled groats; it is grayish, with tiny black specks of hull, and has a strong, earthy taste. Buckwheat flour tends to make baked goods heavier and gives them a distinctive, stronger taste. It is usually blended with other flours. Buckwheat flour is used in pancake mixes, waffles, Russian blinis, Japanese soba noodles (which contain wheat), crêpes, muffins, dumplings, unleavened chapati (an Indian flatbread) and pastries. It can be used as a meat extender in a sausage meat mixture or combined with other GF flours to make breads and quick breads.

Cornmeal is milled from corn. It has larger granules than regular flour and can be yellow, white, red or blue. Although these varieties are slightly different in texture and flavor, one can be substituted for the other. The coarser the grind, the more granular the texture of the finished product and the more intense the corn flavor. Cornmeal can be used to make cornbread or muffins, or it can be cooked and served as a hot cereal. It can also be used as a coating for fried foods or as a meat extender. Cornmeal is sometimes used to dust a greased pan, which helps keep the product from sticking and gives the crust extra crunch and a hint of flavor. **Corn flour** and **cornstarch** are not interchangeable in recipes.

GF Oats are available as groats, rolled oats (oat flakes or oatmeal), oat bran and flour. **Oat flour** is made from finely ground groats, which contain much of the bran. Depending on how it is ground, the flour can be almost as nutritious as the whole grain itself (it is heat during grinding that causes nutrient loss). The high oil content provides a sweet, nutty flavor.

Oat flour makes baked items moist and crumbly, but the products stay fresh longer than items baked with wheat flour. Use it in quick breads, yeast breads, cookies and cakes or to thicken soups, stews, sauces and gravies. Look for oats labeled "pure," "uncontaminated" or "gluten-free."

Millet is not a true grain, but it is closely related to corn and sorghum. It is yellow or white, small and round, with a mild, delicate, corn-like flavor and a texture much like that of brown rice. Millet takes on the flavor of whatever it is cooked with. It can be used in pilafs or casseroles, as a stuffing for vegetables or meat, or in Asian dishes that call for rice, quinoa or buckwheat. We like to add dry millet grain to yeast breads, biscuits and muffins for a crunchy texture.

Quinoa is available as flakes or flour. The **flakes** are whole quinoa kernels rolled flat into flakes that are $1/8$ to $1/4$ inch (3 mm to 0.5 cm) in diameter. Add quinoa flakes to cookie recipes or to replace GF oatmeal or buckwheat flakes in toppings for fruit crisps. **Quinoa flour** is finely ground and tan-colored, with a strong, slightly nutty flavor. Because of its strong flavor, use it in small amounts. Baked products made with quinoa flour have a tender, moist crumb and keep well. We enjoy quinoa flour in pancakes, bread, muffins and crackers.

Rice is available in many forms. **Brown rice flour** is milled from the whole grain. It has a gritty texture and provides more fiber and nutrients than white rice flour. It is only a shade darker than white rice flour and has a mild, nutty flavor. Brown rice flour results in a product with a grainy texture and a fine, dry crumb. Use it in recipes calling for rice flour.

Rice bran and **rice polish** are the two outer parts of the rice kernel that are removed during milling for white rice flour. Rice bran is the outermost layer. Adding bran and polish in small amounts to recipes increases the fiber content. They are interchangeable in recipes.

Sweet rice flour (glutinous rice flour, sticky rice flour) is made from short-grain rice. It contains more starch than brown or white rice flour. There are two grades: one is beige, grainy and sandy-textured; the other is white, starchy, sticky and less expensive. The latter works better in recipes. It is often used to bread foods before frying. We use it to dust baking pans or put some on our fingers for easier handling of sticky dough.

Sorghum is available as a grain, puffed, grits, cracked and flour. The flour ranges in color from a gray-tan to eggshell white, and the grinds vary from coarse (stone-ground) to very fine. Because its flavor is neutral, it absorbs other flavors well. The most wheat-like of all GF flours, it is the best general-purpose flour, giving baked items a warm, creamy color. Sorghum flour adds protein to home-baked goods such as scones, cakes, cookies, breads, muffins,

Fish and Chips (page 80)

pizza dough, waffles, cereals, pastas and chapati. The protein and starch in sorghum endosperm are more slowly digested than those in other grains, making it beneficial for people with diabetes. Some sorghum varieties are so rich in antioxidants, which protect against cell damage, that they are comparable to blueberries (known for their high antioxidant levels).

Teff is available as a grain and a flour. **Teff flour** milled from brown teff has a sweet, nutty, subtle, hazelnut flavor, while flour from white teff is milder. Teff flour has excellent baking qualities. Use it in breads, quick breads, pancakes, waffles, pie crusts, gingerbread, crackers and cookies. It is also a good thickener for soups, sauces, stews, gravies and puddings. Teff is the main ingredient *injera*, the staple bread of Ethiopian cuisine. Due to a low glycemic index, teff is digested slowly, which makes it beneficial for diabetics and athletes.

Storing Gluten-Free Whole Grain Flours

Ingredient	Room Temperature*	Refrigerator	Freezer
Amaranth flour		6 months	1 year
Buckwheat flour		2 months	6 months
Cornmeal/corn flour	1 month	6 months	1 year
Millet flour		6 months	1 year
Rolled oats	2 months		6 months
Oat bran		6 months	1 year
Quinoa flour		6 months	1 year
Rice flours	1 year		1 year
Rice bran, rice polish, brown rice		6 months**	1 year
Sorghum flour	1 month	6 months	1 year
Teff flour	1 month	6 months	1 year

* All gluten-free grains and flours should be stored in airtight containers in a cool, dry, dark place.

** The bran layers in brown rice contain oil that could become rancid; thus, brown rice must be refrigerated.

Other Gluten-Free Baking Ingredients

Fat includes vegetable oil, butter, shortening or margarine. It gives the crust its tenderness and the loaf its softness. It also helps to retain moisture, which keeps the product from staling too quickly. Do not use low-calorie margarine — its high water content will affect the size and texture of the product. Cheese and egg yolk contribute to the fat in some recipes. When measuring shredded cheese, do not pack. Weight is a more accurate measure than volume. If desired, small cubes of cheese can replace shredded, since cheese melts during baking.

Flax seeds (also known as linseed or whole flax seeds) are small, flat and tear-shaped. They range in color from dark reddish-brown to golden brown and have a nutty flavor and a crisp yet chewy texture. **Cracked flax seeds** are not sold in stores, but they can be prepared at home: use a coffee grinder to crack the outer coating of the seed slightly, resulting in pieces of different sizes and textures. Cracked flax seeds are easier to digest than whole. For extra crunch, add slightly cracked flax seeds to yeast breads and quick breads. Refrigerate any extra. **Ground flax seeds** are sold as flax flour, milled flax seeds or sprouted flax flour. All forms of ground flax seeds are interchangeable in recipes. You can prepare your own by grinding whole flax seeds to a golden brown to medium-brown powder with slightly darker flecks. You can add up to 1 tbsp (15 mL) ground flax seeds to the batter for cookies, cakes or pancakes without decreasing the other flours or starches. If you add more, the amount of liquid and other flours may have to be adjusted.

Legume flours (also called pulses) include peas, beans, lentils and peanuts. Besides using dried legumes in our recipes, we also use their flours.

Fava bean flour is made from earthy-flavored fava beans.

Chickpea flour (garbanzo bean flour, gram, besan, chana dal) has a mild, nut-like taste, with a hint of lemon. It adds a rich, sweet flavor to baked foods. It is used in East Indian cuisine and to thicken soups and gravies.

Garfava flour (garbanzo-fava bean flour in Canada) is a blend of garbanzo bean (chickpea) flour and fava bean flour. It has a nutty taste.

Whole bean flour is made from romano beans (cranberry beans or speckled sugar beans). The dried beans are cooked (heat-treated, micronized) to help reduce flatulence, then stone-ground to a uniform, fine, dark, strong-tasting flour. If whole bean flour is not available, any bean or pea flour can be substituted.

Pea flours are produced from dried field peas with the bran (hull) removed. Green pea flour has a sweeter flavor than yellow pea flour. Pea flours keep baked products softer longer and improve dough made in a bread machine. They can be used as a natural colorant in baked goods, homemade noodles and other foods. Pea flours complement recipes made with banana, peanut butter and strong spices such as cloves.

Soy flour (soya flour), made from soybeans, is powdery fine, with a pungent, nutty, slightly bitter flavor that is enhanced by the flavors of accompanying flours. Soy flour is available in full-fat (natural), low-fat and defatted versions. The higher the fat content, the deeper the color. Full-fat soy flour contains the natural oils found in the soybean; defatted soy flour has had the oils removed during processing. Soy flour has a strong odor when wet that disappears with baking. It adds rich color, fine texture, a pleasant nutty flavor, tenderness and moistness to baked goods. Products containing soy flour bake faster and tend to brown quickly, so the baking time may need to be shortened or the oven temperature lowered. Tenting baked goods with foil partway through the baking time also helps. Soy flour can also be used to thicken sauces and gravies, to add a nutty flavor and extra protein to pancake batter and to enrich pasta and breakfast cereals. Added to fried foods such as doughnuts, soy flour reduces the amount of fat absorbed by the dough. Keep in mind that soy is one of the top 10 allergens in Canada and one of the top eight in the U.S. Studies have shown that 15% of those with celiac disease cannot tolerate soybeans or soy products.

Nut flours and meals are made from very finely ground nuts such as almonds, hazelnuts and pecans. They are not as smooth or as fine as grain flours. Nut flours can be purchased, or you can grind them yourself (see the Techniques Glossary, page 217). Grind the nuts when you're ready to prepare the recipe. We like to toast them first, for a nuttier flavor (see page 217). Toasting also dries nut flour, helping to prevent clumping.

Almond flour or **meal** is made from blanched almonds and is creamy white. Sugar or flour is sometimes added during grinding to absorb the oil from the almonds and to prevent clumping, so check purchased almond flour to be sure it is gluten-free. Choose almond flour to combine with rice flour or amaranth flour when a white, delicately flavored product is desired.

Hazelnut flour (hazelnut meal) is a creamy color, with dark brown to black flecks. It has a full, rich flavor that is sweet and nutty. We enjoy it in pastry and anything with orange or chocolate.

Pecan flour (pecan meal) is a warm brown, similar in color to ground flax seeds. It complements recipes made with maple, pumpkin and dried fruits such apricots and dates.

Starches, which are complex carbohydrates, have two purposes in gluten-free cooking: to lighten baked products and to thicken liquids for sauces or gravies.

Baking with Starches

Arrowroot (arrowroot starch, arrowroot powder, arrowroot starch flour) is a fine, white, tasteless starchy powder with a mild aroma. Arrowroot is more expensive and may be more difficult to find than other starches. When mixed with GF flours to make breads, cookies and pastries, arrowroot helps the baked goods bind better and lightens the finished product.

Cornstarch (corn flour, maize, *crème de maïs*) is a fine, silky, white, tasteless starchy powder. When mixed with GF flours to make breads, cookies and pastries, cornstarch helps the baked goods bind better and lightens the finished product.

Potato starch (potato starch flour) is made from only the starch of potatoes, and it is therefore less expensive than potato flour. It is a very fine, silky, white powder with a bland taste. It lumps easily and must be sifted frequently. When combined with other GF flours, it adds moistness to baked goods and gives them a light and airy texture. It also causes breads to rise higher. A permitted ingredient for Passover (unlike cornstarch and other grain-based foods), potato starch is often found with kosher products in supermarkets. Potato starch is often confused with potato flour, but one cannot be substituted for the other.

Tapioca starch (tapioca flour, tapioca starch flour, cassava flour) is powdery fine, white and mildly sweet. Tapioca starch lightens baked goods and gives them a slightly sweet, chewy texture.

Thickening with Starches

All starches can be used to thicken soups, gravies, sauces, stews and meat dishes.

Xanthan gum is a natural carbohydrate produced from the fermentation of glucose. It helps prevent baked goods from crumbling, gives them greater volume, improves their texture and extends their shelf life. It also helps prevent pastry fillings from "weeping," so your crust won't get soggy. Xanthan gum can be purchased at health food stores, online or where you purchase other gluten-free ingredients. Before working with xanthan gum, be sure to wipe counters and containers with a dry cloth; when it comes in contact with water, it becomes slippery, slimy and almost impossible to wipe up.

Do not omit xanthan gum from a recipe, as it is apt to collapse.

Thickener Substitutions

Starch/Flour	To thicken 1 cup (250 mL) of liquid	Cooking Precautions	Cooked Appearance	Tips
Arrowroot	2 tbsp (30 mL)	• add during last 5 minutes of cooking • stir only occasionally • do not boil	• clear shine • glossier than cornstarch	• thickens at a lower temperature than cornstarch • not as firm as cornstarch when cool • doesn't break down as quickly as cornstarch • more expensive • separates when frozen
Cornstarch	2 tbsp (30 mL)	• stir constantly • boil gently for only 1 to 3 minutes	• translucent and shiny	• thickens as it cools • boiling too rapidly causes thinning • boiling for more than 7 minutes causes thinning • add acid (lemon juice) after removing from heat
Potato starch	1 tbsp (15 mL)	• stir constantly	• more translucent and clearer than cornstarch	• lumps easily • thickest at boiling point • thickens as it cools • separates when frozen
Tapioca starch (cassava)	3 tbsp (45 mL)	• add during last 5 minutes of cooking • stir constantly	• transparent and shiny	• dissolves more easily than cornstarch • firms more as it cools • best to use for freezing
Amaranth flour	3 tbsp (45 mL)	• browns quickly and could burn if not watched carefully • thickens at boiling point and slightly more after 5 to 7 minutes of boiling • reheats in microwave	• golden brown color • cloudy, opaque • smooth	• nutty, beefy aroma • if too thick, can be thinned with extra liquid • reheats • excellent for gravy
Potato flour	1 tbsp (15 mL) to 2 tbsp (30 mL)	• mixes well with cold water • cooks quickly without lumps • thickens quickly at lower temperature than cornstarch	• turns transparent after heating	• can be added to sauces at the last minute

Starch/Flour	To thicken 1 cup (250 mL) of liquid	Cooking Precautions	Cooked Appearance	Tips
Rice flour (brown or white)	2 tbsp (30 mL)	• dissolve in cold liquid rather than hot fat or pan drippings • thickens after 5 to 7 minutes of boiling • continues to thicken with extra cooking	• opaque, cloudy • grainy texture • bland flavor	• thickens more as it cools • thickens rapidly when reheated and stirred • stable when frozen
Sorghum flour	2 tbsp (30 mL)	• thickens after 2 to 3 minutes of boiling • does not thicken more with extra cooking	• dull • similar to wheat flour	• thickens as it cools • reheats well on stovetop or in microwave • thickens quickly when extra is added
Sweet rice flour	2 tbsp (30 mL)	• thickens after 5 to 8 minutes of boiling	• shiny, opaque • grainy texture • bland flavor	• thickens as it cools

Guar gum is gluten-free, but it may act as a laxative in some people. It can be substituted for xanthan gum in equal proportions.

Yeast converts the carbohydrates in flour and sugar to produce the carbon dioxide gas that causes dough to rise. The recipes in this cookbook were developed using bread machine (instant) yeast. We always recommend using the type of yeast called for in the recipe. Bread machine (instant) yeast is a very active strain of yeast that can be added directly to the bread machine without the need for preactivating. The expiry date on a package of yeast indicates that it should be opened before that date. Yeast should be kept in an airtight container in the freezer, and there's no need to defrost before measuring. Do not transfer yeast from one container to another; exposing it to air can shorten its life. Perform this test for freshness if you suspect yeast has become less active: Dissolve 1 tsp (5 mL) granulated sugar in 1/2 cup (125 mL) lukewarm water. Add 2 tsp (10 mL) yeast and stir gently. In 10 minutes, the mixture should have a strong yeasty smell and be foamy. If it doesn't, the yeast is too old — time to buy fresh yeast.

Cheese Biscuits (page 130)

Storing Other Gluten-Free Baking Ingredients

Ingredient	Room Temperature*	Refrigerator	Freezer	Additional Information
Flax seeds, whole	1 year			
Flax seeds, cracked or ground		6 months	1 year	For optimum freshness, grind only as needed.
Legume flours		6 months	1 year	
Nut flours and meals**		3 months	1 year	Store away from foods with strong odors such as fish and onions.
Nuts**	6 months		1 year	
Seeds (pumpkin, poppy, sesame and sunflower)**	2 months	6 months	1 year	
Soy flour, full-fat		6 months	1 year	
Soy flour, defatted	1 year			
Starches	Indefinitely			
Xanthan gum and guar gum	6 months		Indefinitely	
Yeast (bread machine and instant)	Not recommended	Not recommended	1 year	Open before expiry date.

* All gluten-free baking ingredients should be stored in airtight containers in a cool, dry, dark place.

** Because of their high oil content, seeds, nuts and nut flours tend to become rancid quickly. Purchase in small quantities and taste before using.

Nutrient Content of Gluten-Free Grains, Flours and Starches

Protein helps us maintain and repair body tissues. Complete proteins (meat, fish, poultry, milk and milk products, eggs) provide all the amino acids necessary for a healthy body; incomplete proteins (grains, legumes, vegetables) lack some of the essential amino acids. However, the body has the ability to use amino acids from a variety of sources to form complete proteins. Here are some suggested combinations: beans and rice, cereals and milk, nuts and grains. Some contain higher levels of essential amino acids than others. It is therefore important to bake with a variety of nutritious grains.

Fat provides the essential fatty acids that the body cannot produce and protects the organs and muscles. Although fats are necessary for a healthy diet, they contain two and a half times as many calories per gram as protein and carbohydrates, so the amount of fat consumed should be controlled.

Carbohydrates are the primary source of energy for the body. They provide fuel as the body breaks down complex carbohydrates into simple sugars.

Fiber is found only in plants. Insoluble fiber aids in digestion, while soluble fiber can lower cholesterol. Sources of insoluble fiber include rice bran, brown rice, almond meal and legumes. Sources of soluble fiber include flax seeds and pears. Oat bran, whole-grain oats and soybeans contain both types. When increasing fiber in the diet, do so gradually. It can result in constipation or diarrhea if increased too quickly.

Calcium helps the body build strong bones and teeth. It is also required for blood clotting, and nerve and muscle function.

Iron is necessary for the formation of hemoglobin in red blood cells. It also helps the immune system function.

Nutrient Content of Gluten-Free Grains, Flours and Starches

Gluten-free product	Protein (g)	Fat (g)	Carbohydrate (g)	Fiber (g)	Calcium (mg)	Iron (mg)
Whole-grain flours						
Amaranth flour	17	8	80	18	51	9.1
Brown rice flour	11	4	124	7	17	3.1
Buckwheat flour	15.14	3.72	84.71	12.0	49	4.87
Cornmeal	9.91	4.38	93.81	8.9	7	4.21
Millet, raw	22.04	8.44	145.7	17.0	16	6.02
Oat flour	21	9	78	12	50	7.2
Quinoa flour	13	8	84	6	61	9.4
Sorghum flour	12	4	88	8	35	5.7
Teff flour	16	4	88	16	201	7.0
Wild rice, cooked	6.54	0.56	35.00	3.0	5	0.98
Wild rice, raw	23.57	1.73	119.84	9.9	34	3.14
Other flours and starches						
Almond flour	24	56	24	12	750	5.4
Cornstarch	0	0	117	1	3	0.6
Flax flour	24	45	38	36	332	7.5
Garfava flour	35	6	72	12	104	7.9
Potato starch	0	0	160	0	0	0
Soy flour (low-fat)	47	6	38	18	241	9.2

Sources: United States Department of Agriculture, Case Nutrition Consulting Inc., Bob's Red Mill, Nu-World Amaranth, Northern Quinoa Corp., Twin Valley Mills and Nutrition Data.

United States Department of Agriculture Agricultural Research Service National Nutrient Database for Standard Reference, Release 28

Using an Instant-Read Thermometer

When we bake gluten-free, it is important to use a thermometer to test foods for doneness since it is more difficult to tell when they are fully baked: the outside of the bread or cake may look browned enough, while the inside is still raw. The indicators you may be used to looking for when baking with wheat may not be reliable because gluten-free foods often have a different appearance. A thermometer is the only accurate way to be sure the food is done.

Purchasing

The best thermometer for this purpose is a bimetallic stemmed thermometer often called an instant-read or chef's thermometer. It has a round head at the top, a long metal stem and a pointed end that senses the temperature. There are both digital and dial versions available. Check the temperature range to be sure it covers the temperatures you need. Instant-read thermometers are widely available in stores and can also be purchased online.

Use

To test baked goods for doneness, insert the metal stem of the thermometer at least 2 inches (5 cm) into the thickest part of what you are baking. With thin or small products, it may be necessary to insert the stem horizontally. Some can be stacked. (A few of the newer thermometers only need to be inserted to a depth of ¾ inch (2 cm), so check the manufacturer's instructions.) Gluten-free baked goods, whether breads, cakes or muffins, are baked at 200°F (100°C). Do not leave the thermometer in during baking: the plastic cover will melt, ruining the thermometer.

Cleaning

Be sure to clean the probe thoroughly after each use, and store the thermometer in the plastic sleeve, if available. Some of the more expensive ones (but not all) are dishwasher-safe. Make sure to read the manufacturer's instructions.

Buckwheat Pancakes with
Mixed Grill (page 44)

Nanaimo Bars (page 150)

Speaking Our Language: Are We All on the Same Page?

"GF" means "gluten-free," such as GF sour cream, GF oat bran, etc., when both gluten-free and gluten-containing products are available. We recommend that you read package labels every time you purchase a GF product. Manufacturers frequently change the ingredients.

Keeping the following points in mind as you prepare our recipes will help you get the same great results we did:

- Rather than using a standard mix of flours in our recipes, we like to vary the proportions of flours and starches so that each recipe has a unique flavor and texture. We love the results we get when we use a mixture of sorghum flour and bean flour with strong flavors such as pumpkin, chocolate, molasses, dates and rhubarb. We selected specific GF flour combinations for individual recipes based on the desired texture and flavor of the final product. Unless mentioned as a variation, we have not tested other GF flours in the recipes. Substituting other flours may adversely affect the results.

- GF recipes can be temperamental. Even an extra tablespoon (15 mL) of water in a loaf of bread can cause the recipe to fail. Use a graduated, clear, liquid measuring cup for all liquids. Place it on a flat surface and read it at eye level.

- Select either metric or imperial measures and stick to that for the whole recipe: do not mix.

- Select the correct dry measures (e.g., $\frac{1}{2}$ cup and $\frac{1}{4}$ cup when the recipe calls for $\frac{3}{4}$ cup, or 125 mL and 50 mL for 175 mL). For accuracy and perfect products, use the "spoon lightly, heap and level once" method of measuring. For small amounts, use measuring spoons, not kitchen cutlery. (Long-handled, narrow measuring spoons made especially to fit spice jars are accurate and fun to use.)

- We used large eggs, liquid honey, light (fancy) molasses, bread machine (instant) yeast, unsweetened fruit juice (not fruit drinks) and salted butter. We know you'll get the same great results if you bake with these, but expect slightly different results if you make substitutions.

- We tested with 2%, 1% or nonfat milk, yogurt and sour cream, but our recipes will work with other fat levels.

- Unless otherwise stated in the recipe or in your bread machine manual, eggs and dairy products are used cold from the refrigerator. If the manufacturer recommends warming the eggs and heating the liquid to a specific temperature, be sure to follow their directions or the loaf will be short and raw in the middle.

- All foods that require washing are washed before preparation. Foods such as bananas are peeled, but apples, rhubarb and zucchini are not (unless specified).

- If the preparation method (chopped, melted, diced, sliced) is listed before the food, it means that you prepare the food before measuring. If it is listed after the food, measure first, then prepare. Examples are "melted butter" versus "butter, melted"; "ground flax seeds" versus "flax seeds, ground"; and "cooked quinoa" versus "quinoa, cooked."

- If in doubt about a food term, a piece of equipment or a specific recipe technique, refer to the glossaries (pages 209 to 218) at the back of the book.

Classic French Onion Soup

Soups and Salads

Broccoli and Cheese Soup 29

Chicken Noodle Soup 30

Cream of Mushroom Soup 32

Classic French Onion Soup 33

New England Clam Chowder 34

Caesar Salad with Dijon Dressing 36

Garlic Croutons 37

Pasta Salad 38

Blue Cheese Dressing 40

Raspberry Pecan Vinaigrette 41

Tips for Making Soup

- It is very easy to double and triple soup recipes and so wonderful to have lots in the freezer, so always plan to make larger quantities. When ready, cool to room temperature by sitting the pot in a sink of cold water, stirring occasionally. Cover and refrigerate overnight until completely cold. You may want to leave some in the fridge, but be sure to eat it within 3 days. Freeze the rest in convenient-size containers. Soup will keep in the freezer for 2 months.

- When chopping vegetables, consider if they can fit onto a spoon and be eaten easily. Don't forget kale and spinach need to be chopped well or they will be difficult to eat without wearing your soup.

- To ensure a flavorful soup, sweat vegetables like onions, celery, carrots and garlic. This involves cooking in oil or butter over low heat until completely softened.

- Add vegetables that take the longest to cook first and the shortest to cook last. Celery and carrots take longer than peppers and peas, for example.

- Good flavorful stock is one of the most important ingredients when making clear soups. You can purchase or make your own. Check for gluten in commercial stocks, broths and cubes.

- Simmering rather than boiling is also important when cooking to retain flavor and texture. Vegetables can become mushy; meat and seafood can become tough.

- Remember, any canned or packaged GF ingredients usually have a lot of salt in them already; therefore, we don't like to use extra salt. If necessary, we prefer to add it at the end, after tasting.

- If you have an immersion blender, use it to quickly purée soups.

- Warming milk or cream before adding it to cream soups will help prevent curdling. Once it's in the pot, make sure not to bring the liquid to a boil or it could curdle. You want the soup to resemble the thickness of whipping cream.

- Use these general guidelines when serving soup: 1 cup (250 mL) for appetizers; $1\frac{1}{3}$ to $1\frac{1}{2}$ cups (325 to 375 mL) for a main course.

Broccoli and Cheese Soup

Makes 4 servings

The popularity of this recipe crept up on us and it has become a favorite of many. Some folks like it with a little crunchiness — which the addition of chopped broccoli florets provides — and so do we.

Tips

Peel broccoli stems if they are woody. Woody stems are thick and heavy for their size and can have hollow parts.

GF vegetable broth can be used for a vegetarian version of this soup.

4 oz (125 g) cheese = 1 cup (250 mL) shredded.

For a chunky style soup, don't purée in food processor or blender.

- • Food processor or blender

2 tsp	vegetable oil	10 mL
2	cloves garlic, minced	2
1 cup	finely grated carrots	250 mL
1/2 cup	finely chopped onion or shallots	125 mL
1 tbsp	butter	15 mL
2 tbsp	teff flour	30 mL
2 1/2 cups	GF chicken broth	625 mL
2 cups	diced broccoli stalks and florets	500 mL
1 tbsp	chopped fresh thyme	15 mL
2 cups	chopped broccoli florets	500 mL
1/4 tsp	dry mustard	1 mL
1 cup	shredded sharp (old) Cheddar cheese	250 mL
	Salt and freshly ground white pepper	

1. In a large saucepan, heat oil over medium heat. Add garlic, carrots and onion. Cook, stirring frequently, until vegetables are tender, but not browned. Transfer vegetables to food processor or blender.

2. In same saucepan, add butter; sprinkle with teff flour, stir, and cook 2 to 3 minutes or until the consistency of dry sand. Slowly whisk in chicken broth and then add diced broccoli stalks and florets. Simmer, covered, for 10 to 15 minutes or until broccoli is tender.

3. In food processor or blender, purée in batches. Return to saucepan. Add thyme and chopped broccoli florets. Simmer until broccoli is tender. Stir in dry mustard and Cheddar cheese.

4. Season to taste with salt and white pepper; serve.

Nutrients per serving

Calories	243
Fat	16 g
Saturated fat	8 g
Cholesterol	33 mg
Sodium	717 mg
Carbohydrate	14 g
Fiber	4 g
Protein	13 g
Calcium	270 mg
Iron	2 mg

Variations

Substitute cauliflower for all or part of the broccoli.

Try basil, marjoram or tarragon instead of the thyme.

Substitute sorghum flour for the teff.

1 tsp (5 mL) dried thyme can be used instead of fresh.

Use a different cheese: Emmental works as a good substitute for Cheddar.

Chicken Noodle Soup

Makes 4 servings

Whenever you don't feel well, chicken noodle soup hits the spot like nothing else will. It soothes colds and warms the soul. Our recipe is much healthier than the canned variety; it's lower in sodium and has no MSG or preservatives.

Tips

You can use GF vermicelli or GF stick noodles for this recipe. Use ½ cup (125 mL) uncooked noodles or broken up vermicelli for every 2 cups (500 mL) chicken broth.

Chicken can be left over from another meal or cooked fresh for the soup.

This recipe can be doubled or tripled. Refrigerate for up to 3 days or freeze for up to 2 months.

2 tsp	olive oil	10 mL
2 tsp	dried thyme	10 mL
2	medium carrots, diced	2
2	stalks celery, thinly sliced	2
1	medium onion, diced	1
3 cups	GF chicken broth	750 mL
¾ cup	GF noodles	175 mL
1 cup	cooked chicken, cut into bite-size pieces	250 mL
	Salt and white pepper	

1. Heat a large saucepan over medium-low heat. Add olive oil and swirl to coat surface of pan. Add thyme, carrots, celery and onion. Cook, stirring frequently, for 5 to 10 minutes until soft and translucent, but not brown. Transfer to a bowl and set aside.

2. In same saucepan, bring chicken broth to a boil. Add noodles, return to a boil and cook, for 2 to 3 minutes, until noodles are al dente. Add chicken and reserved vegetables.

3. Heat through, season to taste with salt and pepper; serve.

Variations

You can vary the pasta shape for a change: both tortellini or farfalle work well.

To make soup heartier, add some chewy cooked grains — either 1 cup (250 mL) rice or quinoa — instead of or in addition to the noodles.

Nutrients per serving

Calories	253
Fat	5 g
Saturated fat	1 g
Cholesterol	27 mg
Sodium	624 mg
Carbohydrate	37 g
Fiber	2 g
Protein	15 g
Calcium	55 mg
Iron	2 mg

Cream of Mushroom Soup

Makes 4 servings

The real benefit to making your own mushroom soup is the deeper, richer flavor you achieve using the different varieties of mushrooms. It is delicious!

Tips

Choose different varieties of mushrooms depending on what's available; white, brown, cremini (firmer and with a stronger flavor than regular white button), portobello caps (mature cremini with a strong concentrated flavor), shiitake and oyster all work nicely.

The correct way to clean mushrooms is to wipe them with a slightly damp paper towel or cloth and then dry well. They will brown better.

Initially, the mushrooms will release quite a bit of moisture, which will evaporate, and then mushrooms will brown.

Nutrients per serving

Calories	170
Fat	12 g
Saturated fat	7 g
Cholesterol	29 mg
Sodium	481 mg
Carbohydrate	10 g
Fiber	2 g
Protein	8 g
Calcium	90 mg
Iron	1 mg

3 tbsp	butter, divided	45 mL
1/4 cup	onion, finely chopped	60 mL
3/4 lb	sliced assorted mushrooms	335 g
2 tbsp	teff flour	30 mL
2 cups	GF chicken broth	500 mL
1/2 tsp	dried thyme	2 mL
1 cup	whole milk	250 mL
	Salt and white pepper	

1. In a saucepan, melt 1 tbsp (15 mL) butter over medium heat; add onion and mushrooms. Cook, stirring occasionally, for 15 to 20 minutes or until mushrooms are browned and tender, and onion is soft. Transfer vegetables to a bowl and set aside.

2. In same saucepan, melt remaining 2 tbsp (30 mL) butter. Add teff flour, stir, and cook for 2 to 3 minutes or until the consistency of dry sand.

3. Slowly whisk in chicken broth and thyme; bring to a boil. Reduce heat to medium-low and simmer for 10 to 15 minutes. Add milk and heat gently until steaming. Do not let boil or soup may curdle. Season to taste with salt and pepper. Serve.

Variations

Just before serving, add 3 tbsp (45 mL) dry sherry.

For a heartier soup, add 1/2 cup (125 mL) wild rice with the chicken broth and simmer gently for 40 minutes before adding milk.

Substitute dried tarragon for the thyme.

Substitute sorghum or amaranth flour for the teff flour.

GF vegetable broth can be used for a vegetarian version of this soup.

Classic French Onion Soup

Makes 8 servings

Our families love French onion soup! Because it can be a bit time consuming to make, we like to make a big batch to freeze, so that it's on hand to serve for lunch when friends or relatives drop in. This soup brings back fond memories of cold winter Saturday lunches.

Tips

This soup can be made ahead up to the end of Step 3. Let cool, transfer to an airtight container and refrigerate for up to 2 days. Reheat over medium heat until steaming, then proceed with Step 4.

Don't try to rush when browning the onions. The longer and slower they are cooked, the richer and deeper the flavor of the soup. The length of time to brown can take longer; it all depends on the size and the shape of the saucepan.

Nutrients per serving

Calories	259
Fat	11 g
Saturated fat	5 g
Cholesterol	21 mg
Sodium	818 mg
Carbohydrate	33 g
Fiber	4 g
Protein	8 g
Calcium	151 mg
Iron	1 mg

• Eight 1½-cup (375 mL) ovenproof bowls or ramekins

2 tbsp	butter	30 mL
1 tbsp	vegetable oil	15 mL
6 cups	thinly sliced onions	1.5 L
1 tsp	granulated sugar	5 mL
2 tbsp	sorghum or teff flour	30 mL
8 cups	GF beef broth	2 L
8	thick slices GF bread, cubed	8
1 cup	shredded Swiss cheese	250 mL
2 tbsp	freshly grated Parmesan cheese	30 mL

1. In a large saucepan, melt butter over low heat. Add vegetable oil and onions; cook, stirring occasionally, for about 15 minutes or until soft and transparent.

2. Stir in sugar and cook, stirring frequently, for 50 to 60 minutes or until onions are deep golden brown.

3. Stir in sorghum flour and cook, stirring constantly, for 3 minutes. Gradually stir in beef broth and bring to a boil. Reduce heat to medium-low and simmer, stirring occasionally, for 30 minutes.

4. Meanwhile, preheat broiler. Place ovenproof bowls on a baking sheet. Divide soup among bowls. Evenly top each bowl with bread cubes and sprinkle with Swiss cheese and Parmesan cheese. Broil until cheeses are bubbly and lightly browned. Serve.

Variations

Vary the onion; try yellow, red or part leeks. Yellow onions have a stronger flavor and odor, which causes the eyes to water more. Red onions will be milder and sweet, and leeks are subtle and milder, as well.

For the GF bread, use GF Mock Pumpernickel (page 101) or GF Brown Sandwich Bread (page 100).

Some folks like to use aged Cheddar, Emmental and/or Gruyère in place of the Swiss cheese.

Stir in ½ cup (125 mL) Madeira, dry white wine or dry sherry just before ladling the soup into bowls. It will give the soup a deeper, richer flavor.

Substitute 8 slices of GF bread for the GF bread cubes.

New England Clam Chowder

Makes 6 servings

For those of us raised inland, this classic is a rare treat. It's well worth the road trip to the coast if you can, or make your own.

Tips

In Canada a tin of baby clams is 284 g (9 oz) net weight; 142 g drained weight. Each 284 g tin yields $2/3$ cup (150 mL) baby clams and 1 cup (250 mL) juice. Three 9 oz (284 g) tins is approximately 2 cups (500 mL) of clams.

In the USA, a $6\frac{1}{2}$ oz (185 g/190 mL) tin of clam meat yields $\frac{1}{2}$ cup (125 mL) of clam meat pieces, drained, plus $\frac{1}{2}$ cup (4 oz/125 mL) of juice.

Use low temperature after the clams are added because high heat makes the clam meat tough.

2 tbsp	butter	30 mL
1	medium onion, finely chopped	1
1	stalk celery, chopped	1
2 tbsp	amaranth flour	30 mL
3	tins (each 9 oz/284 g) baby clams with broth	3
2 cups	russet potatoes, diced	500 mL
1	bay leaf	1
2 cups	half-and-half (10%) cream	500 mL
	Salt and white pepper	
3	slices GF bacon, cooked crisp and crumbled	3

1. In a large saucepan, melt butter over medium heat. Add onion and celery, and cook about 4 minutes or until softened. Whisk in amaranth flour and cook, stirring constantly, for 1 to 2 minutes.

2. Stir clams, including broth, into onion-celery mixture. Add potatoes and bay leaf; bring to a boil. Reduce heat, cover and simmer for 15 minutes or until potatoes are tender.

3. Slowly stir in cream; heat over low heat until steaming. Remove bay leaf and season to taste with salt and pepper. Do not allow to boil or chowder may curdle. Garnish with GF bacon. Serve with extra cream on the side for folks to add if they find chowder too thick for their taste.

Variations

Add all ingredients to a large (6 to 8 quart) slow cooker and cook on low for 3 to 4 hours.

To make this a seafood chowder, add 2 cups (500 mL) cooked shrimp, cooked white fish and scallops with the cream. Heat until steaming and shrimp, white fish and scallops are hot.

Nutrients per serving

Calories	344
Fat	19 g
Saturated fat	10 g
Cholesterol	146 mg
Sodium	831 mg
Carbohydrate	21 g
Fiber	1 g
Protein	26 g
Calcium	256 mg
Iron	33 mg

Caesar Salad with Dijon Dressing

Makes 4 servings

Once considered to be only served in restaurants, Caesar salad has become more popular than tossed green salad in our homes today.

Tips

Leftover salad dressing can be stored in the refrigerator for up to 6 weeks. It's also delicious on steamed vegetables, such as Brussels sprouts.

For a milder mustard flavor, reduce the Dijon mustard to 1 tbsp (15 mL).

If you find the dressing too tart for your taste, substitute water for part of the lemon juice or add 2 tsp (10 mL) liquid honey.

Dijon Dressing

¾ cup	extra virgin olive oil	175 mL
⅓ cup	freshly squeezed lemon juice	75 mL
2 to 3 tbsp	Dijon mustard	30 to 45 mL

Salad

1	head romaine lettuce, torn into bite-size pieces	1
½ cup	freshly grated Parmesan cheese	125 mL
4	slices GF bacon, cooked crisp and crumbled	4
	Garlic Croutons (page 37)	
	Freshly ground pepper	

1. *Dijon Dressing:* In a small bowl, whisk together olive oil, lemon juice and Dijon mustard to taste. Set aside for at least 1 hour before serving to allow flavors to develop and blend.

2. *Salad:* In a large bowl, combine enough lettuce and just enough dressing to moisten greens.

3. Top salad with Parmesan cheese, bacon and Garlic Croutons. Season to taste with pepper. Serve.

Variation

Rather than mixing the dressing in a small bowl, add the ingredients to a glass jar or bottle with a tight-fitting lid. Then it can be shaken to mix the ingredients.

Nutrients per serving

Calories	483
Fat	47 g
Saturated fat	8 g
Cholesterol	18 mg
Sodium	531 mg
Carbohydrate	9 g
Fiber	3 g
Protein	9 g
Calcium	165 mg
Iron	2 mg

Garlic Croutons

Makes 4 dozen croutons (6 servings)

Use these to top any salad, but they are traditional and particularly tasty on a Caesar salad.

Tips

Croutons are a good way to use up stale leftover gluten-free bread. It also can be made into bread crumbs.

You can freeze bread cubes right before the bread goes stale. Store in a freezer bag or container and remove them from the freezer as needed. Defrost at room temperature while you prepare the rest of the recipe, then add.

- Preheat oven to 375°F (190°C)
- Rimmed baking sheet

4	slices day-old GF bread, cut into 1-inch (2.5 cm) cubes	4
1 tbsp	extra virgin olive oil	15 mL
2	cloves garlic, minced	2

1. In a bowl, toss bread cubes with olive oil and garlic. Spread in a single layer on baking sheet. Bake in preheated oven, turning frequently, for 10 to 15 minutes or until crisp and golden. Cool completely, then store in an airtight container.

Variations

Add dried herbs, such as thyme, marjoram or rosemary.

Make croutons from the White, Brown or Mock Pumpernickel bread recipes on pages 96, 100 or 101.

Nutrients per serving (8 croutons)

Calories	95
Fat	4 g
Saturated fat	0 g
Cholesterol	0 mg
Sodium	80 mg
Carbohydrate	14 g
Fiber	1 g
Protein	1 g
Calcium	2 mg
Iron	1 mg

Pasta Salad

Makes 4 servings

There is nothing like having a pasta salad ready in the refrigerator for family and drop-in guests. Just add some salmon or tuna for a quick luncheon salad.

Tips

1 cup (250 mL) small pasta weighs approx. ¼ lb (125 g).

The pasta is rinsed in Step 1 to stop the cooking process.

If fresh herbs are not available, use one-third the amount of dried herbs.

This salad can be prepared up to 3 days ahead and stored in the refrigerator in an airtight container. The flavors improve over time.

Pasta Salad

¼ lb	GF macaroni, penne or fusilli	125 g
½ cup	dry-packed sun-dried tomatoes	125 mL
½ cup	chopped green onions	125 mL
½ cup	chopped celery	125 mL
½ cup	chopped fresh parsley	125 mL
½ lb	crumbled feta cheese	250 g
1 to 2 tbsp	freshly grated Parmesan cheese	15 to 30 mL
¾ cup	pitted and sliced kalamata olives	175 mL

Vinaigrette

2 tbsp	white balsamic vinegar	30 mL
2 tbsp	freshly squeezed orange juice	30 mL
2 tbsp	extra virgin olive oil	30 mL
2 tsp	Dijon mustard	10 mL
2 tbsp	each, fresh basil and fresh thyme, chopped	30 mL
	Salt and white pepper	

1. *Pasta Salad:* In a large saucepan of boiling water, cook macaroni for 6 to 8 minutes or until al dente. Rinse with cold water and drain well. Set aside to cool.

2. In a large bowl, combine pasta, sun-dried tomatoes, onions, celery, parsley, feta cheese, Parmesan cheese and olives.

3. *Vinaigrette:* In a small bowl, whisk together vinegar, orange juice, olive oil, mustard, basil and thyme.

4. Pour vinaigrette over salad and stir to combine. Season to taste with salt and pepper. Serve.

Variation

Add ½ cup (125 mL) rinsed drained chickpeas, substitute grape tomatoes for sun-dried tomatoes and add 3 cups (750 mL) packed baby spinach. Use GF fusilli, rotini or small shelled pasta for the GF macaroni.

Nutrients per serving

Calories	415
Fat	24 g
Saturated fat	10 g
Cholesterol	52 mg
Sodium	1177 mg
Carbohydrate	34 g
Fiber	2 g
Protein	13 g
Calcium	344 mg
Iron	3 mg

Blue Cheese Dressing

Makes ¾ cup (175 mL) dressing (1 tbsp/15 mL per serving)

This is one of our all-time favorites. It goes great with spinach, romaine lettuce and chicken wings.

Tip

Purchase lemons on sale. Zest and juice, then freeze separately for later use when you are in a hurry.

½ cup	canola oil	125 mL
2 tbsp	white vinegar	30 mL
2 tbsp	freshly squeezed lemon juice	30 mL
1 tsp	granulated sugar	5 mL
¼ tsp	salt	1 mL
Dash	white pepper	Dash
¼ tsp	dry mustard	1 mL
2 oz	crumbled GF blue cheese	60 g

1. Whisk together canola oil, vinegar, lemon juice, sugar, salt, pepper and mustard; add blue cheese. Let stand 20 minutes to allow flavors to develop. Refrigerate in an airtight container for up to 4 days.

Variations

Substitute extra virgin olive oil for all or part of the canola oil.

Substitute liquid honey for the sugar.

Nutrients per serving

Calories	106
Fat	11 g
Saturated fat	1 g
Cholesterol	4 mg
Sodium	119 mg
Carbohydrate	1 g
Fiber	0 g
Protein	1 g
Calcium	27 mg
Iron	0 mg

Raspberry Pecan Vinaigrette

Makes 1 cup (250 mL) vinaigrette

(1 tbsp/15 mL per serving)

We like to make our own salad dressings, which are healthier and more economical than processed alternatives. We use healthy oils and little or no salt and sugar, so we know there are no chemical additives.

Tip

Don't have a blender or food processor? Use a glass bowl or 4-cup (1 L) measure and whisk ingredients together. Make sure you don't use an aluminum bowl, though: the acid in the vinegar reacts with the metal, leaving the dressing with a metallic taste. You could also use a glass jar or bottle with a tight-fitting lid and shake the ingredients.

- Food processor or blender
- Fine-mesh sieve

½ cup	fresh or frozen raspberries	125 mL
¼ cup	raspberry-flavored balsamic vinegar	60 mL
1 to 3 tbsp	pure maple syrup	15 to 45 mL
⅓ cup	extra virgin olive oil	75 mL
1 tbsp	Dijon mustard	15 mL
¼ cup	chopped pecans	60 mL

1. *To make raspberry purée:* Using the back of a spoon, press raspberries through fine-mesh sieve, discarding seeds. Be sure to scrape off and add the part that remains on the underside of the sieve. The purée will look like slightly thickened juice. This will yield approximately 3 tbsp (45 mL).

2. Using food processor or blender, combine raspberry purée, vinegar, maple syrup, olive oil and mustard. Process until smooth. Let stand 20 minutes to allow flavors to develop. Process again and add pecans. Refrigerate in an airtight container for up to 4 days.

Variations

Seedless raspberry jam can be used for part or all of the raspberry purée.

White pepper and a dried herb can be added; try oregano, thyme or marjoram.

Substitute pecan oil for the olive oil.

Use a raspberry-flavored, plain white or red wine vinegar for the raspberry-flavored balsamic vinegar.

Nutrients per serving

Calories	61
Fat	6 g
Saturated fat	1 g
Cholesterol	0 mg
Sodium	24 mg
Carbohydrate	2 g
Fiber	0 g
Protein	0 g
Calcium	5 mg
Iron	0 mg

Hearty Beef Stew
with Biscuit Topping

Entrées and Sides

Buckwheat Pancakes with Mixed Grill 44

Classic Buttermilk Waffles 46

Classic Thin Pizza Crust Two Ways. 48

Vegetarian Pizza 50

Traditional All-Dressed Pizza 52

Hawaiian Pizza. 53

Mac 'n' Cheese 54

Spaghetti and Meatballs 56

Lasagna 58

Cheese Soufflé 60

Microwave Meatloaf 61

Hearty Beef Stew with Biscuit Topping 62

Veal Parmesan. 64

Tourtière 66

Tacos 68

Taco Seasoning. 69

Oven-Fried Chicken 70

Roast Turkey 72

Poultry Stuffing 74

Turkey Gravy 75

Chicken Pot Pie. 76

Chicken Fingers 78

Fish and Chips 80

Salmon Patties 82

Coconut Shrimp 84

Seafood Fettuccine. 86

Quiche Lorraine 87

Scalloped Potatoes. 88

Cheese Sauce for Veggies 90

Cream Sauce. 91

Buckwheat Pancakes with Mixed Grill

Makes 8 pancakes (1 per serving)

Don't let the title fool you! Buckwheat is nutritious, gluten-free, flavorful and colorful, too. We like to serve these with a mixed grill for either lunch, brunch or a light supper. If you grow your own tomatoes, bring in green tomatoes before the first frost, wrap individually in newspaper and store in a dark, cool place. You will have a supply to last all fall.

Tip

For information on determining when your griddle is hot enough, see the Techniques Glossary, Skillet page 217.

Nutrients per serving

Calories	273
Fat	13 g
Saturated fat	4 g
Cholesterol	58 mg
Sodium	752 mg
Carbohydrate	19 g
Fiber	2 g
Protein	21 g
Calcium	110 mg
Iron	2 mg

- Griddle or nonstick skillet, lightly greased
- Electric hand mixer

Mixed Grill

8	GF Italian sausages, mild or hot	8
8	GF bacon slices	8
4	large green tomatoes, thickly sliced (see Tips, at left)	4

Buckwheat Pancakes

1/3 cup	buckwheat flour	75 mL
1/3 cup	sorghum flour	75 mL
2 tbsp	cornstarch	30 mL
2 tsp	granulated sugar	10 mL
1/2 tsp	xanthan gum	2 mL
2 tsp	GF baking powder	10 mL
1 tsp	baking soda	5 mL
1/4 tsp	salt	1 mL
1	egg	1
1 cup	buttermilk	250 mL
1 tbsp	vegetable oil	15 mL

1. *Mixed Grill:* With a fork, prick sausages in several places. In medium saucepan, add $1/2$ to $3/4$ inch (1 to 2 cm) water and sausages. Cover and cook over low heat for 15 to 20 minutes or until instant-read thermometer registers 160°F (71°C).

2. Meanwhile, lay bacon slices, not overlapping, in a large, deep, cold skillet. Cook over medium-low heat, turning when strips begin to curl. Cook, turning frequently, for 7 to 8 minutes or until golden brown and crisp. Place on a plate lined with paper towels. Cover with a second layer of paper towels and blot. Set aside and keep warm.

3. Heat prepared griddle over medium-high heat.

4. Drain off any collected fat from bacon, leaving enough fat to just coat bottom of skillet. Add cooked sausages and turn frequently to brown evenly. Place on paper towel–lined plate. Set aside and keep warm. Add tomatoes to skillet and cook just until beginning to soften, about 3 to 5 minutes.

5. *Buckwheat Pancakes:* Meanwhile, in a large bowl or plastic bag, combine buckwheat flour, sorghum flour, cornstarch, sugar, xanthan gum, baking powder, baking soda and salt. Mix well and set aside.

6. In a bowl, using electric hand mixer, beat egg, buttermilk and vegetable oil until combined. Add dry ingredients and mix until almost smooth with a few lumps remaining.

7. For each pancake, pour $\frac{1}{4}$ cup (60 mL) batter onto prepared griddle and cook for about 3 minutes or until the bottom is deep golden and the top surface wrinkles around edges. Turn and cook for 30 to 60 seconds longer or until bottom is golden. Repeat with the remaining batter, lightly greasing griddle between batches, as necessary, wiping off excess.

8. *Assembly:* Serve 1 sausage, 1 slice bacon and one-eighth of tomato slices with each pancake.

Variations

If you don't have fluid buttermilk on hand, use 1 cup water (250 mL) and $\frac{1}{3}$ cup (75 mL) buttermilk powder. Add buttermilk powder to dry ingredients in Step 1. Add water in Step 2.

If you don't have green tomatoes, ripe tomatoes work well, too.

Classic Buttermilk Waffles

Makes about 6 waffles (1 per serving)

Most of us think of waffles for breakfast on the weekends, but why not for brunch or a light supper? Any leftover waffles can be frozen and enjoyed for another meal.

Tips

Most new electric hand mixers have a wire whisk attachment, which will give you a better beating action, but a standard hand mixer works well, too.

The batter should be thick — don't add extra liquid.

For a lighter waffle, warm egg whites before beating (see Techniques Glossary, page 217).

Wrap cooked waffles well and freeze for up to 1 month. Separate layers with waxed paper. Reheat in a toaster or toaster oven.

- Electric hand mixer fitted with wire whisk attachment (see Tips, at left)
- Waffle maker, lightly greased, then preheated

½ cup	sorghum flour	125 mL
½ cup	teff flour	125 mL
¼ cup	potato starch	60 mL
¼ cup	buttermilk powder	60 mL
2 tbsp	granulated sugar	30 mL
½ tsp	xanthan gum	2 mL
2¼ tsp	GF baking powder	11 mL
¾ tsp	baking soda	3 mL
Pinch	salt	Pinch
2	eggs, separated	2
¾ cup	water	175 mL
2 tbsp	vegetable oil	30 mL

1. In a large bowl or plastic bag, combine sorghum flour, teff flour, potato starch, buttermilk powder, sugar, xanthan gum, baking powder, baking soda and salt. Mix well and set aside.

2. In a small bowl, using electric hand mixer, beat egg whites until stiff but not dry. Set aside.

3. In a separate bowl, using electric hand mixer, beat egg yolks, water and vegetable oil until combined. Add dry ingredients and beat until smooth. Fold in egg whites.

4. Pour in enough batter to fill preheated waffle maker two-thirds full. Close lid and cook for 6 to 8 minutes or until no longer steaming. Repeat with the remaining batter.

Variations

Use ¾ cup (175 mL) fluid buttermilk for water and buttermilk powder.

Add ½ cup (125 mL) blueberries, chopped apple or nuts to batter.

Serve with Oven-Fried Chicken (page 70) for a more decadent meal.

Nutrients per serving

Calories	208
Fat	7 g
Saturated fat	1 g
Cholesterol	65 mg
Sodium	214 mg
Carbohydrate	30 g
Fiber	3 g
Protein	6 g
Calcium	175 mg
Iron	2 mg

Classic Thin Pizza Crust Two Ways

Makes 2 crusts
(6 servings per pizza)

The thickness of pizza crust is a personal preference. Our favorite is right-to-the-edge thin-crust pizza.

Tips
Don't worry about the cracks on the surface of this crust after 12 to 15 minutes of baking.

Expect slight shrinkage from edges.

- Preheat oven to 400°F (200°C)
- Two 12-inch (30 cm) pizza pans, lightly greased

Bread Machine Method

1 cup	sorghum flour	250 mL
1 cup	whole bean flour	250 mL
1/3 cup	tapioca starch	75 mL
1 tsp	granulated sugar	5 mL
1/2 tsp	xanthan gum	2 mL
1 1/2 tsp	bread machine or instant yeast	7 mL
1 tsp	salt	5 mL
1 tsp	dried oregano	5 mL
1 3/4 cups	water	425 mL
1 tsp	cider vinegar	5 mL
2 tbsp	vegetable oil	30 mL

1. In a large bowl or plastic bag, combine sorghum flour, whole bean flour, tapioca starch, sugar, xanthan gum, yeast, salt and oregano. Mix well and set aside.

2. Pour water, vinegar and oil into bread machine baking pan. Select Dough Cycle. Gradually add dry ingredients as bread machine is mixing, scraping the sides with a rubber spatula while adding. Try to incorporate all dry ingredients within 1 to 2 minutes. Allow bread machine to complete the cycle.

3. Immediately pour onto prepared pans. Spread evenly with a water-moistened rubber spatula. Let rise in a warm, draft-free place for 15 minutes. Bake in preheated oven for 12 to 15 minutes or until firm.

4. Spread with your choice of toppings (see recipes on pages 50, 52 and 53). Return to oven and bake according to recipe topping directions.

Nutrients per serving

Calories	112
Fat	3 g
Saturated fat	0 g
Cholesterol	0 mg
Sodium	197 mg
Carbohydrate	18 g
Fiber	3 g
Protein	4 g
Calcium	16 mg
Iron	1 mg

Tip
This dough can be divided into equal portions to make eight 6-inch (15 cm) individual pizzas. Bake on greased baking sheets for 10 to 12 minutes.

Variation
Use 1 tbsp (15 mL) chopped fresh oregano for dried herb.

Mixer Method
• Stand mixer fitted with paddle attachment

1 cup	sorghum flour	250 mL
1 cup	whole bean flour	250 mL
1/3 cup	tapioca starch	75 mL
1 tsp	granulated sugar	5 mL
1/2 tsp	xanthan gum	2 mL
1 1/2 tsp	bread machine or instant yeast	7 mL
1 tsp	salt	5 mL
1 tsp	dried oregano	5 mL
1 3/4 cups	room temperature water	425 mL
1 tsp	cider vinegar	5 mL
2 tbsp	vegetable oil	30 mL

1. In a large bowl or plastic bag, combine sorghum flour, whole bean flour, tapioca starch, sugar, xanthan gum, yeast, salt and oregano. Mix well and set aside.

2. In mixer bowl, combine water, vinegar and vegetable oil until well blended. With mixer on the lowest speed, slowly add dry ingredients until combined. With a rubber spatula, scrape the bottom and sides of bowl. With mixer on medium speed, beat for 1 minute or until smooth.

3. Immediately pour onto prepared pans. Spread evenly with a water-moistened rubber spatula. Let rise in a warm, draft-free place for 15 minutes. Bake in preheated oven for 12 to 15 minutes or until firm.

4. Spread with your choice of toppings (see recipes on pages 50, 52 and 53). Return to oven and bake according to recipe topping directions.

Vegetarian Pizza

Makes 1 pizza (6 servings)

We like lots of topping with every bite of pizza, and this pizza has lots of them. You can increase or decrease the amount of vegetables to suit your tastes.

Tip

If the partially baked pizza crust is frozen, defrost wrapped crust on the counter for 30 minutes before topping.

- Preheat oven to 400°F (200°C)

1	recipe Classic Thin Pizza Crust (page 48), partially baked	1
3 tbsp	extra virgin olive oil	45 mL
2 tbsp	minced garlic	30 mL
3 to 4	plum (Roma) tomatoes, thinly sliced	3 to 4
1	large yellow or orange bell pepper, thinly sliced	1
1½ cups	sliced cremini mushrooms	375 mL
1 cup	broccoli florets	250 mL
½ cup	thinly sliced red onions	125 mL
1 cup	shredded mozzarella cheese	250 mL
½ cup	freshly grated Parmesan cheese	125 mL

1. Brush olive oil over crust to within ¼ inch (0.5 cm) of the edges. Sprinkle with garlic. Arrange tomatoes, yellow pepper, mushrooms, broccoli and red onions over top. Sprinkle with mozzarella and Parmesan cheeses. Bake in preheated oven for 20 to 25 minutes or until crust is brown and crisp, vegetables are soft and cheese is bubbly.

2. Transfer to a cutting board, let cool slightly and cut into 6 slices. Serve immediately. Transfer any extra slices to a wire rack to prevent crust from getting soggy.

Variation

Choose other vegetables for toppings: cooked spinach, blanched thin asparagus, roasted butternut squash, eggplant, caramelized onions, leeks, fennel, arugula or thinly sliced zucchini all work well.

Nutrients per serving

Calories	296
Fat	17 g
Saturated fat	5 g
Cholesterol	21 mg
Sodium	423 mg
Carbohydrate	25 g
Fiber	4 g
Protein	12 g
Calcium	199 mg
Iron	2 mg

Traditional All-Dressed Pizza

Makes 1 pizza (6 servings)

Most folks would say they grew up with this topping on their pizza when they ordered for home delivery.

Tips

A pizza wheel makes cutting pizza simple.

Cut into bite-size pieces to serve as appetizers for a party.

Purchase or make your own GF pizza sauce.

• Preheat oven to 400°F (200°C)

1	recipe Classic Thin Pizza Crust (page 48), partially baked	1
¾ cup	Pizza Sauce (variation, page 57)	175 mL
1 cup	GF pepperoni slices	250 mL
⅓ cup	red onion slices	75 mL
1	medium red bell pepper, coarsely chopped	1
1 cup	mushrooms, sliced	250 mL
1½ cups	mozzarella cheese, shredded	375 mL

1. Spread sauce over crust to within $\frac{1}{4}$ inch (0.5 cm) of the edges. Top with pepperoni, red onion, red pepper, mushrooms and mozzarella cheese. Bake in preheated oven for 20 to 25 minutes or until crust is brown and crisp and cheese is bubbly.

2. Transfer to a cutting board, let cool slightly and cut into 6 slices. Serve immediately. Transfer any extra slices to a wire rack to prevent crust from getting soggy.

Variations

Substitute freshly grated Parmesan cheese for part of mozzarella.

You may also want to use any of these additional toppings: bacon, sausage, tomato slices, black olives, green olives, artichoke, anchovy, green bell pepper.

Nutrients per serving

Calories	176
Fat	7 g
Saturated fat	1 g
Cholesterol	8 mg
Sodium	368 mg
Carbohydrate	23 g
Fiber	4 g
Protein	7 g
Calcium	39 mg
Iron	2 mg

Hawaiian Pizza

**Makes 1 pizza
(6 servings)**

This pizza is Donna's grandson's favorite. He is not fond of spicy meats such as pepperoni and salami, but he does love the ham and pineapple combination.

Tips

A pizza wheel makes cutting pizza simple.

Cut into bite-size pieces to serve as appetizers for a party.

Purchase or make your own GF pizza sauce.

• **Preheat oven to 400°F (200°C)**

1	recipe Classic Thin Pizza Crust (page 48), partially baked	1
¾ cup	Pizza Sauce (variation, page 57)	175 mL
1½ cups	cubed GF cooked ham	375 mL
1 cup	drained canned pineapple tidbits	250 mL
¾ cup	thinly sliced green bell pepper	175 mL
1½ cups	shredded mozzarella cheese	375 mL

1. Spread sauce over crust to within ¼ inch (0.5 cm) of the edges. Sprinkle with ham, pineapple, green pepper and mozzarella cheese. Bake in preheated oven 20 to 25 minutes or until cheese is bubbly and crust is golden.

2. Transfer to a cutting board, let cool slightly and cut into 6 slices. Serve immediately. Transfer any extra slices to a wire rack to prevent crust from getting soggy.

Variations

Use Asiago or provolone cheese for mozzarella.

GF barbecue sauce can be used for GF pizza sauce, and 1½ cups (375 mL) cooked cubed chicken can be used for cooked cubed ham.

Nutrients per serving

Calories	307
Fat	14 g
Saturated fat	5 g
Cholesterol	49 mg
Sodium	868 mg
Carbohydrate	27 g
Fiber	4 g
Protein	21 g
Calcium	184 mg
Iron	2 mg

Mac 'n' Cheese

Makes 6 servings

This is the granddaddy of all comfort foods — a favorite of all grandchildren, both young and old. They love it from the time they can finger feed themselves sitting in a highchair.

Tips

If you prefer a milder cheese flavor, use a less aged Cheddar cheese.

Make sure not to pack cheese when measuring.

4 oz (125 g) cheese = 1 cup (250 mL) shredded; 2 oz (60 g) = ½ cup (125 mL) shredded.

You can prepare unbaked Mac 'n' Cheese ahead of time; refrigerate for up to 2 days then bake.

Mac 'n' Cheese can also be cut into portion-size servings, wrapped airtight and frozen for up to 6 weeks.

Nutrients per serving

Calories	277
Fat	18 g
Saturated fat	11 g
Cholesterol	48 mg
Sodium	299 mg
Carbohydrate	19 g
Fiber	2 g
Protein	10 g
Calcium	304 mg
Iron	1 mg

- Preheat oven to 350°F (180°C)
- 8-cup (2 L) microwave-safe measuring cup or bowl
- 8-inch (20 cm) square baking dish, lightly greased

Crumb Topping

3 tbsp	fresh GF bread crumbs	45 mL
2 tsp	melted butter	10 mL
2 tbsp	freshly grated Parmesan cheese	30 mL

Pasta and Cheese Sauce

1 cup	GF elbow pasta	250 mL
3 tbsp	butter	45 mL
3 tbsp	amaranth flour	45 mL
¼ tsp	dry mustard	1 mL
1½ cups	milk	375 mL
1½ to 1¾ cups	shredded extra-sharp (extra-old) or sharp (old) Cheddar cheese	375 to 425 mL
	Salt and freshly ground pepper to taste	

1. *Crumb Topping:* In a small bowl, combine bread crumbs, butter and Parmesan cheese. Set aside.

2. *Pasta and Cheese Sauce:* In a large saucepan, cook pasta in boiling water according to package instructions, just until tender. Drain well. Set aside.

3. In a large microwave-safe measuring cup, microwave butter on High for 1 to 2 minutes or until melted. Stir in amaranth flour and dry mustard. Microwave on High for 4 to 5 minutes or until mixture is the consistency of dry sand, stirring twice. Gradually stir in milk. Microwave on High for 5 to 7 minutes, stirring 2 to 3 times until mixture comes to a boil and thickens. Season with salt and pepper. Stir in Cheddar cheese until melted. Add pasta and gently stir until combined.

4. Pour into prepared baking dish. Sprinkle with crumb topping. Bake for 20 to 30 minutes or until hot and crumb topping is golden in color.

Variations

Vary the shape of pasta: try small shells, penne, elbows, rotini or small bows.

Try a combination of Cheddar, Swiss and Parmesan cheeses.

Evaporated milk or a nut milk can be used for cow's milk.

Spaghetti and Meatballs

**Makes 6 servings
(36 meatballs)**

How convenient it is to have meatballs at the ready when you're short on time! Just pop them frozen into a sauce to defrost and reheat at the same time.

Tips

This recipe can be easily doubled or tripled.

For instructions on making bread crumbs, see the Techniques Glossary, page 216.

Meatballs will be more tender if handled gently and not overmixed.

If you don't have time to make your own pasta sauce, purchase sauce that is GF. Sizes of sauce containers vary from 21 to 23 oz (621 to 680 mL).

Nutrients per serving

Calories	444
Fat	6 g
Saturated fat	2 g
Cholesterol	82 mg
Sodium	687 mg
Carbohydrate	69 g
Fiber	6 g
Protein	25 g
Calcium	161 mg
Iron	7 mg

- Preheat oven to 400°F (200°C)
- 15- by 10-inch (38 by 25 cm) rimmed baking sheet, lightly greased

Pasta Sauce

4	garlic cloves, minced	4
2	large onions, chopped	2
3	sweet bell peppers, seeded, chopped	3
2	cans (28 oz/796 mL) tomatoes with juices	2
4	large bay leaves	4
2 tbsp	dried basil	30 mL
1 tbsp	dried thyme	15 mL
2 tsp	granulated sugar	10 mL

Meatballs

1/3 lb	lean ground beef	165 g
1/3 lb	lean ground veal or chicken	165 g
1/3 lb	ground pork	165 g
1	egg, slightly beaten	1
1/4 cup	fine dry GF bread crumbs	60 mL
2 tbsp	fresh marjoram	30 mL
2 tbsp	tomato paste	30 mL
1/2 tsp	salt	2 mL
1/4 tsp	freshly ground black pepper	1 mL
3/4 lb	GF spaghetti	375 g

1. *Pasta Sauce:* In a large saucepan, over medium heat, cook garlic and onions until garlic starts to brown and onions are soft and translucent, 8 to 10 minutes. Add peppers and cook until slightly soft, 8 to 10 minutes. Add tomatoes and crush with a spoon or potato masher. Add bay leaves, basil, thyme and sugar. Bring to a boil, reduce heat to medium-low and simmer for 2 to 2½ hours until most of the liquid has evaporated or until desired consistency. Remove bay leaves.

2. *Meatballs:* Meanwhile, in a large bowl, combine ground beef, ground veal, ground pork, egg, bread crumbs, marjoram, tomato paste, salt and pepper. Mix gently with a fork.

Tips

You can substitute 10 to 12 (2 lb/1 kg) fresh peeled tomatoes for each 28 oz (796 mL) tin of tomatoes.

In a hurry? Simmer pasta sauce for a shorter time and add tomato paste, 1 tbsp (15 mL) at a time, until desired thickness.

It's easy to freeze meatballs on a baking sheet. Once frozen, transfer meatballs to a heavy-duty freezer bag and seal bag. Freeze for up to 2 months. Remove meatballs — as needed — and add directly to sauce just before serving. They will heat through quickly.

Store extra sauce in airtight containers for up to 4 days in the fridge or 6 months in the freezer.

2 oz (60 g) dry spaghetti = 2 servings = 1 cup (250 mL) cooked spaghetti — roughly the diameter of a quarter.

Be sure to check pasta before end of cooking time because it's very easy to overcook GF pasta.

3. Shape into 1-inch (2.5 cm) balls. Place in a single layer on prepared baking sheet. Bake in preheated oven for 15 to 20 minutes or until no longer pink in the center.

4. Meanwhile, in a pot over high heat, bring 16 to 20 cups (4 to 5 L) of water to a boil. Add spaghetti. Bring back up to a boil; lower heat to medium. Boil uncovered, stirring occasionally, for 10 minutes or until just tender or al dente. Drain well.

5. Add meatballs to 3 to $3\frac{1}{2}$ cups (750 to 875 mL) pasta sauce and heat thoroughly (see Tips, at left). Serve over cooked GF spaghetti.

Variations

Use 1 lb (500 g) lean ground beef, ground chicken, ground veal or ground pork for the combination in recipe.

If fresh marjoram is not available, use one-third the amount of dried marjoram. Oregano, basil or rosemary would also be good substitutes.

To turn pasta sauce into pizza sauce: In Step 4, add 2 tbsp (30 mL) dried oregano and 2 tsp (10 mL) marjoram, and if desired, 2 tsp (10 mL) ground fennel seeds. Simmer for an additional hour or until desired thickness.

Lasagna

Makes 8 to 9 servings

This is the ideal dish to make for a crowd — just watch to see how fast it disappears.

Tips

Either make your own pasta sauce or purchase one that is gluten-free. Sizes vary from 21 to 23 oz (621 to 680 mL).

To save time, purchase 7 oz (210 g) shredded mozzarella cheese and use it all in this recipe.

We found that, for each layer, 3 noodles lengthwise and 1 crosswise fit nicely in pan without overlapping.

Be sure noodles in each layer are completely covered with beef mixture.

Freeze leftover lasagna in individual portions for up to 1 month. Thaw and reheat in the microwave 10 to 15 minutes before serving.

Nutrients per serving

Calories	374
Fat	12 g
Saturated fat	6 g
Cholesterol	111 mg
Sodium	674 mg
Carbohydrate	33 g
Fiber	5 g
Protein	32 g
Calcium	304 mg
Iron	6 mg

- Preheat oven to 350°F (180°C)
- 13- by 9-inch (33 by 23 cm) baking pan

1½ lbs	lean ground beef	750 g
1	onion, diced	1
4 cups	Pasta Sauce (page 56)	1 L
1½ cups	water	375 mL
1 cup	cottage cheese	250 mL
2	eggs, lightly beaten	2
12	GF oven-ready lasagna noodles	12
5 oz	baby spinach	150 g
2 cups	shredded mozzarella cheese	500 mL
½ cup	freshly grated Parmesan cheese	125 mL

1. In a large skillet over medium heat, cook beef and onion, breaking beef up with a fork, for 5 minutes or until beef is browned and onion is tender. Drain off fat.

2. Add Pasta Sauce and water to beef mixture and bring to a boil. Reduce heat and simmer for 10 minutes. Set aside.

3. In a small bowl, combine cottage cheese and eggs. Set aside.

4. Spread a thin layer of beef mixture in baking pan. Top with 4 lasagna noodles, making sure they don't overlap. Cover with one-third of the remaining beef mixture, half spinach and half cottage cheese mixture. Sprinkle with half mozzarella cheese. Cover with 4 lasagna noodles and layer with half the remaining beef mixture, remaining spinach and remaining cottage cheese mixture and mozzarella cheese. Cover with the remaining lasagna noodles, beef mixture and Parmesan cheese. Cover with foil.

5. Bake in preheated oven for 1 hour. Remove foil and bake for 15 minutes or until bubbly, noodles are cooked and cheese is golden brown. Let stand for 10 to 15 minutes before serving.

Variation

Substitute tomato juice or garden vegetable juice for water for a richer sauce with a stronger tomato flavor.

Cheese Soufflé

Makes 4 servings

This savory French dish was once thought to be very difficult to prepare. Today, we are more relaxed about making a soufflé. Ask your guests to be seated before the dish is ready to come out of the oven, and that way everyone will be able to see it when it's high and gorgeous — and before it deflates!

Tips

See the Equipment Glossary, page 210, for information on soufflé dishes.

Use Cheddar, Swiss, Asiago, Gruyère, a commercial mix or a combination of these for 2 cups (500 mL) shredded cheese.

The soufflé can be completely prepared, covered and refrigerated for up to 4 hours before baking.

Nutrients per serving

Calories	457
Fat	36 g
Saturated fat	21 g
Cholesterol	279 mg
Sodium	697 mg
Carbohydrate	9 g
Fiber	1 g
Protein	24 g
Calcium	527 mg
Iron	2 mg

- Preheat oven to 300°F (150°C)
- Electric hand mixer fitted with wire whisk attachment
- 10-cup (2.5 L) soufflé dish, at least 3 inches (7.5 cm) deep, buttered

¼ cup	butter	60 mL
¼ cup	amaranth flour	60 mL
1 cup	milk	250 mL
2 cups	shredded cheese (see Tips, at left)	500 mL
½ tsp	dry mustard	2 mL
¼ tsp	salt	1 mL
¼ tsp	paprika	1 mL
Pinch	cayenne pepper	Pinch
4	eggs, separated	4
¼ tsp	cream of tartar	1 mL

1. In a microwave-safe bowl, microwave butter on High for 1 to 2 minutes or until melted.

2. Stir in amaranth flour and microwave on High for 1 to 2 minutes or until mixture is the consistency of dry sand. Stir in milk and microwave on High for 3 to 5 minutes, stopping to stir occasionally, until mixture comes to a boil and has thickened. Stir in cheese, mustard, salt, paprika and cayenne pepper. Set aside.

3. In a small bowl, using electric hand mixer, beat egg yolks for 5 minutes or until thick and lemon colored. Fold in cheese mixture.

4. In a large bowl, using electric hand mixer fitted with clean wire whisk attachment, beat egg whites and cream of tartar until stiff but not dry. Fold in cheese mixture. Spoon into prepared soufflé dish.

5. Bake in preheated oven for 60 to 75 minutes or until puffed and golden brown. Be sure not to open the oven door during baking or the soufflé will deflate. Serve immediately.

Variations

Try shredded extra-sharp (extra-old) Cheddar cheese in place of mix of cheeses.

Substitute 1 tbsp (15 mL) Dijon mustard for dry mustard.

Microwave Meatloaf

Makes 6 servings

Hungry for dinner? Try this recipe with a side of garlic bread, a salad and baked apple for dessert.

Tip

The meatloaf will have a much better and lighter texture if you handle ground beef gently when mixing and spooning into pan.

- Microwave-safe 10-inch (25 cm) tube pan, ungreased

Sauce

½ cup	tomato sauce	125 mL
2 tbsp	packed brown sugar	30 mL
2 tbsp	freshly squeezed lemon juice	30 mL
1 tbsp	prepared mustard	15 mL

Loaf

1½ lb	ground beef	750 g
½ cup	tomato sauce	125 mL
½ cup	GF oats	125 mL
¼ cup	chopped onion	60 mL
1	egg, beaten	1
½ tsp	salt	2 mL
¼ tsp	freshly ground pepper	1 mL

1. *Sauce:* In a small bowl, combine tomato sauce, brown sugar, lemon juice and mustard. Set aside.

2. *Loaf:* In a large bowl, combine beef, tomato sauce, oats, onion, egg, salt and pepper. Spoon into tube pan.

3. Cover with waxed paper; microwave on High for 10 minutes. Drain fat.

4. Spread sauce on meatloaf. Microwave on High for 10 minutes or until internal temperature registers 160°F (71°C) on instant-read thermometer. Let stand 10 minutes, covered with foil, shiny side in.

Variations

Substitute ⅓ cup (75 mL) dry GF bread crumbs for oatmeal.

Use ground turkey, chicken, veal or pork for all or some of ground beef.

Use GF store-bought pizza sauce for tomato sauce for added flavor.

Alternatively, bake in a 9- by 5-inch (23 by 12.5 cm) loaf pan at 350°F (180°C) for 1 to 1¼ hours or until an instant-read thermometer registers 160°F (71°C).

Nutrients per serving

Calories	251
Fat	8 g
Saturated fat	3 g
Cholesterol	101 mg
Sodium	525 mg
Carbohydrate	17 g
Fiber	2 g
Protein	28 g
Calcium	35 mg
Iron	4 mg

Hearty Beef Stew with Biscuit Topping

Makes 6 to 8 servings

Enjoy this dish for dinner on a cold winter's night — there will be enough left over for another meal.

Tip

If you have access to a cast-iron Dutch oven, use for this recipe.

- Cheesecloth
- Kitchen string
- 5- to 7-quart Dutch oven
- Food processor

Beef Stew

2	bay leaves	2
2 tsp	whole black peppercorns	10 mL
1 tsp	whole cloves	5 mL
½ tsp	whole allspice	2 mL
1 to 3 tbsp	vegetable oil	15 to 45 mL
2 to 3 lbs	stewing beef	1 to 1.5 kg
2	parsnips, cut into 2-inch (5 cm) pieces	2
2	potatoes, cut into 2-inch (5 cm) pieces	2
3	cloves garlic	3
1	small turnip, peeled and thinly sliced	1
1	onion, cut into wedges	1
1	large carrot, peeled and cut into 1-inch (2.5 cm) pieces	3
¼	butternut squash, peeled and cut into 2-inch (5 cm) pieces (about 1 cup/250 mL)	¼
1	can (28 oz/796 mL) diced tomatoes, with juice	1
½ cup	GF beef broth	125 mL
¼ cup	tomato paste	60 mL
	Salt and freshly ground black pepper	
¼ cup	sorghum flour	60 mL
2 tbsp	vegetable oil	30 mL

Biscuit Topping

1 tbsp	freshly squeezed lemon juice or white vinegar	15 mL
1 cup	milk	250 mL
1 cup	sorghum flour	250 mL
⅓ cup	whole bean flour	75 mL
¼ cup	tapioca starch	60 mL
1 tbsp	granulated sugar	15 mL
1 tsp	xanthan gum	5 mL
1 tbsp	GF baking powder	15 mL
½ tsp	baking soda	2 mL
¼ tsp	salt	1 mL
3 tbsp	vegetable oil	45 mL

Nutrients per serving

Calories	483
Fat	18 g
Saturated fat	3 g
Cholesterol	73 mg
Sodium	686 mg
Carbohydrate	50 g
Fiber	9 g
Protein	34 g
Calcium	234 mg
Iron	4 mg

Variations

Use one-half an acorn squash for butternut.

Substitute 3 to 4 lbs (1.5 to 2 kg) less-tender beef roast, cut into 1-inch (2.5 cm) cubes, for stewing beef.

To make a vegetarian stew, substitute 2 cans (19 oz/540 mL) kidney beans or black beans, rinsed and drained, for stewing beef.

1. *Beef Stew:* In a 6-inch (15 cm) square piece cheesecloth, place bay leaves, peppercorns, cloves and allspice. Tie with kitchen string and set aside.

2. In large Dutch oven, heat 1 tbsp (15 mL) vegetable oil over medium heat. Brown beef in batches, adding oil as needed between batches. Drain off fat and return all beef to pan. Add parsnips, potatoes, garlic, turnip, onion, carrot and squash. Top with tomatoes with juice, broth and tomato paste. Add spice bag.

3. Bring to a boil over medium-high heat. Immediately reduce heat to low and simmer gently, stirring occasionally, for 1 to 1½ hours or until beef is tender. Discard spice bag. Season to taste with salt and pepper.

4. In a small bowl, combine sorghum flour and oil. Stir into stew, increase heat to medium and simmer for about 15 minutes or until thickened.

5. Preheat oven to 425°F (220°C).

6. *Biscuit Topping:* To sour milk: stir together lemon juice and milk, set aside for 5 minutes.

7. Meanwhile, in food processor, pulse sorghum flour, whole bean flour, tapioca starch, sugar, xanthan gum, baking powder, baking soda and salt until combined. In a separate bowl, whisk together vegetable oil and sour milk mixture. With motor running, gradually add oil mixture to food processor through feed tube in a steady stream. Process for 5 to 10 seconds or until dough just holds together. Do not overprocess.

8. Drop biscuit topping by heaping spoonfuls onto hot stew. Bake for 15 to 20 minutes or until tops are golden. Serve immediately.

Veal Parmesan

Makes 4 servings

This is another entrée that can be quickly prepared on a weeknight. Serve over spaghetti, add some greens and garlic bread, and dinner is ready.

Tips

4 veal cutlets weigh approximately 1 lb (500 g).

If cutlets are not of even thickness, with a sharp knife, butterfly the thick portion. Then cutlets will cook in the same amount of time. See the Techniques Glossary, page 216, for information on how to butterfly.

If you are using leftover pasta sauce cold from the fridge, warm to room temperature in the microwave before topping cutlets.

- Deep 12-inch (30 cm) skillet

½ cup	sweet rice flour	125 mL
2	eggs	2
1 cup	cornmeal	250 mL
1 tsp	dried basil	5 mL
1 tsp	garlic powder	5 mL
1 tsp	dried oregano	5 mL
1 tsp	dried thyme	5 mL
½ tsp	dried rosemary	2 mL
1 lb	veal cutlets	500 g
1 to 2 tbsp	vegetable oil	15 to 30 mL
¾ cup	GF pasta sauce	175 mL
1	cup shredded mozzarella cheese	250 mL
¼ cup	freshly grated Parmesan cheese	60 mL

1. Place sweet rice flour in a shallow dish or plastic bag. Set aside.

2. In a pie plate or shallow dish, beat eggs. Set aside.

3. In a shallow dish or plastic bag, combine cornmeal, basil, garlic powder, oregano, thyme and rosemary. Set aside.

4. Dredge each veal cutlet first in sweet rice flour, then in egg and then in cornmeal mixture. In skillet, heat oil over medium heat. Fry cutlets for 2 to 3 minutes on each side or until browned.

5. Top each with approximately 3 tbsp (45 mL) pasta sauce and sprinkle evenly with mozzarella and Parmesan cheese. Cover and cook until cheese is melted and sauce is hot.

Variations

Vary the herbs used to make Italian seasoning: try sage, cilantro, marjoram, parsley, onion powder, red pepper flakes and pepper. Omit the ones you don't like.

Use either homemade or commercial GF pasta sauce.

Nutrients per serving

Calories	590
Fat	26 g
Saturated fat	10 g
Cholesterol	194 mg
Sodium	459 mg
Carbohydrate	52 g
Fiber	3 g
Protein	35 g
Calcium	259 mg
Iron	4 mg

Tourtière

Makes 2 tourtières (12 to 16 servings)

The tradition in French-Canadian households is to serve tourtière on Christmas Eve. Some families wait to eat until after candlelight church service. It's very easy to share.

Tips

If you want to freeze and bake later, complete up to the end of Step 6, wrap airtight and freeze. Bake from frozen in a preheated 375°F (190°C) oven for 60 to 75 minutes or until crust is golden and internal temperature of filling registers 160°F (71°C) on instant-read thermometer.

Slits in top crust allow steam to escape.

Nutrients per serving

Calories	803
Fat	47 g
Saturated fat	21 g
Cholesterol	196 mg
Sodium	591 mg
Carbohydrate	77 g
Fiber	4 g
Protein	20 g
Calcium	40 mg
Iron	2 mg

- 4- to 6-quart Dutch oven
- Two 9-inch (23 cm) pie plates

2 lb	ground pork	1 kg
½ lb	ground beef	225 g
2	small onions, finely chopped	2
1	small clove garlic, minced	1
¾ tsp	celery seeds	3 mL
½ tsp	ground cinnamon	2 mL
¼ tsp	ground cloves	1 mL
¼ tsp	salt	1 mL
½ cup	water	125 mL
½ cup	fresh GF bread crumbs	125 mL
4	recipes Classic Pastry (page 180), unbaked	4

1. In large Dutch oven, over medium heat, brown ground pork and ground beef. Drain off fat, reserving ¼ cup (60 mL), and add back to pot with meat. Add onions, garlic, celery seed, cinnamon, cloves, salt, water and bread crumbs. Cook uncovered over medium-low heat for 1½ hours, stirring frequently to allow flavors to meld.

2. Cool to lukewarm, about 1 hour.

3. Preheat oven to 450°F (230°C).

4. Roll out pastry for a double-crust pie between two sheets of parchment paper. Carefully remove top sheet of parchment paper and invert pastry over pie plate, easing it in. Carefully peel off remaining sheet of parchment paper.

5. Divide meat mixture evenly and spoon filling into unbaked pie shell. Moisten edge of pastry with water. Carefully remove top sheet of parchment paper from top pastry, invert and cover filling. Carefully peel off the remaining sheet of parchment paper. Trim pastry, leaving ¾-inch (2 cm) overhang. Fold overhang under bottom pastry rim, seal and flute edge.

6. Cut numerous $\frac{1}{2}$-inch (1 cm) slits near the center of pie through crust to filling or cut out a 1-inch (2.5 cm) circle in the center of crust.

7. Bake in preheated oven for 10 to 15 minutes; reduce to 350°F (180°C) and bake for 30 to 40 minutes longer until crust is golden and internal temperature of filling registers 160°F (71°C) on instant-read thermometer. Let cool for 10 to 15 minutes before serving.

Variation
Use all ground pork, beef, veal, chicken or a part of each.

Tacos

Makes 4 servings

There's nothing like tacos for a speedy mid-week supper. We like to double the recipe and have enough for a second night.

Tip

This recipe can be easily doubled or tripled.

• Deep 12-inch (30 cm) skillet or large saucepan

1 lb	ground beef	500 g
1 cup	water	250 mL
⅓ cup	Taco Seasoning (page 69)	75 mL
8 to 12	GF taco shells	8 to 12
	Shredded lettuce (optional)	
	Chopped fresh tomatoes (optional)	
	GF sour cream (optional)	
	GF salsa (optional)	
	Shredded cheese (optional)	

1. In large skillet over medium heat, cook beef, breaking up with a fork, for 5 minutes or until browned and no pink remains. Drain off fat. Add water and taco seasoning. Stir to combine. Bring to a boil and immediately reduce heat to low and simmer for 15 to 20 minutes, stirring occasionally, to allow flavors to combine.

2. Serve with a GF taco shell and shredded lettuce, chopped fresh tomatoes, GF sour cream, GF salsa and your favorite shredded cheese, if desired.

Variation

Use ground chicken, turkey or veal for all or part of ground beef. Vary toppings to suit chosen meat.

Nutrients per serving

Calories	314
Fat	12 g
Saturated fat	4 g
Cholesterol	70 mg
Sodium	234 mg
Carbohydrate	22 g
Fiber	3 g
Protein	27 g
Calcium	59 mg
Iron	4 mg

Taco Seasoning

Makes 1 cup (250 mL) (2 tbsp/30 mL per serving)

Unable to find a gluten-free, salt-free taco seasoning? Here's the answer.

Tips

Check to be sure all seasonings are fresh and gluten-free.

We use about 2 tbsp/30 mL per serving.

Extra taco seasoning can be stored in the freezer for up to 1 year. There is no need to thaw or warm to room temperature before use.

½ cup	dried minced onion	125 mL
¼ cup	chili powder	60 mL
4 tsp	tapioca starch	20 mL
4 tsp	garlic powder	20 mL
4 tsp	ground cumin	20 mL
2 tsp	dried oregano	10 mL
½ tsp	cayenne pepper	2 mL

1. In a small bowl, combine onion, chili powder, tapioca starch, garlic powder, cumin, oregano and cayenne. Mix well.

2. Store in an airtight container in a cool, dry place for up to 1 year.

Variations

Cornstarch or potato starch can be used for tapioca starch.

To make this corn-free, use potato starch not potato flour.

Increase or decrease chili powder and cayenne pepper according to the amount of heat you prefer.

To further increase heat, add hot pepper flakes to taste.

Nutrients per serving

Calories	44
Fat	1 g
Saturated fat	0 g
Cholesterol	0 mg
Sodium	70 mg
Carbohydrate	9 g
Fiber	3 g
Protein	1 g
Calcium	40 mg
Iron	1 mg

Oven-Fried Chicken

Makes 4 servings

Fried chicken is a favorite of many families for Sunday night dinner. This recipe offers a safer, healthier preparation method.

Tips

To crush GF corn flakes, place between two layers of waxed paper and roll with a rolling pin.

Poultry seasoning is a combination of marjoram, thyme, sage, rosemary and sometimes includes nutmeg and pepper. Vary the herbs used, if desired.

- Preheat oven to 350°F (180°C)
- Baking sheet, lined with foil, shiny side down

1 cup	GF corn flakes, crushed	250 mL
1 tbsp	GF poultry seasoning	15 mL
2	egg yolks	2
1/4 cup	milk	60 mL
4	small boneless skinless chicken breasts	4

1. In a shallow dish or plastic bag, combine corn flakes and poultry seasoning. Set aside.

2. In a small bowl, whisk together egg yolks and milk. Set aside.

3. Butterfly each chicken breast and pat dry (see Techniques Glossary, page 216).

4. Dip chicken pieces into egg mixture, then into corn flakes seasoning mixture and press to completely cover.

5. Place on prepared baking sheet. Bake in center of preheated oven for 30 to 45 minutes or until crispy outside, juices run clear and chicken is 170°F (77°C) when measured with instant-read thermometer.

Variations

Use 1 to 1 1/4 lbs (500 g to 570 g) boneless skinless chicken legs or thighs for breasts.

Add 1 tbsp (15 mL) each of Dijon mustard and honey to egg yolks.

Nutrients per serving

Calories	197
Fat	6 g
Saturated fat	2 g
Cholesterol	169 mg
Sodium	199 mg
Carbohydrate	8 g
Fiber	0 g
Protein	27 g
Calcium	47 mg
Iron	3 mg

Roast Turkey

**12-lb (5.5 kg)
GF turkey, frozen,
allowing 1 lb
(500 g)/person**

Everyone enjoys turkey
for the holidays, but it
can easily be prepared
for other occasions as
well. We like to make
our own stuffing bread
(page 98), so we wanted
to share the whole
process of this true
classic comfort food.

Tip

For a quicker defrosting
method, cover turkey with
cold water (the sink is a
good place for this). Change
with fresh cold water every
30 minutes; allow 1 hour
per pound (500 g).

- Large, shallow roasting pan with rack
- Oven-safe meat thermometer
- GF turkey, frozen, allowing 1 lb (500 g)/person

1. Thaw turkey in original wrapper in the fridge. Allow for
   five hours per pound (500 g).

2. Remove small bag of giblets and the neck from inside bird.
   Rinse and dry the cavity with paper towels.

3. Preheat oven to 325°F (160°C).

4. Truss turkey (see Techniques Glossary, page 216).

5. Place turkey, breast side up, on rack in roasting pan. Insert
   oven-safe thermometer into the thickest part of the thigh,
   being careful it does not touch the bone.

6. Tent with foil (see Techniques Glossary, page 216).

7. Roast turkey in preheated oven. See box (page 73) for
   approximate roasting times, and roast until thermometer
   registers 180°F (90°C) in thigh and 170°F (80°C) in breast.

8. Remove foil for the last hour of cooking.

9. Remove turkey from oven and allow turkey to rest, tenting
   loosely with foil for 15 to 20 minutes before carving.

Nutrients per 4-oz
serving of cooked
turkey

Calories	193
Fat	6 g
Saturated fat	2 g
Cholesterol	86 mg
Sodium	79 mg
Carbohydrate	0 g
Fiber	0 g
Protein	33 g
Calcium	28 mg
Iron	2 mg

Tips

The United States Department of Agriculture (USDA), and Agriculture and Agri-Food Canada both recommend baking stuffing separately, not inside turkey.

You can rub some sage and savory on the inside of turkey or add onions, celery, carrots, lemon wedges or orange wedges.

Tenting turkey with foil and letting it stand before carving allows the juices at the surface to distribute evenly throughout the meat, resulting in a more tender meat.

Your roasting pan needs to be big enough so that the turkey fits inside completely, with at least an inch (2.5 cm) of space between it and the sides. Three inches (7.5 cm) high is generally a good height for the sides to hold all the drippings.

Roasting Times

Weight	Unstuffed
6 to 8 lbs (3 to 3.5 kg)	$2\frac{1}{2}$ to $2\frac{3}{4}$ hours
8 to 10 lbs (3.5 to 4.5 kg)	$2\frac{3}{4}$ to 3 hours
10 to 12 lbs (4.5 to 5.5 kg)	3 to $3\frac{1}{4}$ hours
12 to 16 lbs (5.5 to 7 kg)	$3\frac{1}{4}$ to $3\frac{1}{2}$ hours
16 to 22 lbs (7 to 10 kg)	$3\frac{1}{2}$ to 4 hours

* Canadian Turkey Marketing Agency

Poultry Stuffing

Makes 12 to 14 cups (3 to 3.5 L)

(1 cup/250 mL per serving)

Baking stuffing outside the bird will still have the traditional flavor, but you can control the moistness, which ensures your stuffing won't be dry when you serve it.

Tips

Allow 1 cup (250 mL) stuffing for each 1 lb (500 g) raw poultry.

Recipe can be halved depending on the size of the turkey.

Stuffing can be made up to 2 days ahead of time, refrigerated and reheated in oven while turkey is resting.

A 1.5-lb (750 g) loaf yields approximately 12 to 14 cups (3 to 3.5 L) bread cubes.

Nutrients per serving

Calories	151
Fat	5 g
Saturated fat	1 g
Cholesterol	27 mg
Sodium	333 mg
Carbohydrate	24 g
Fiber	4 g
Protein	4 g
Calcium	79 mg
Iron	2 mg

1	loaf Stuffing Bread (page 98)	1
2 cups	chopped celery	500 mL
1 cup	chopped onions	250 mL
1 cup	GF chicken broth	250 mL
1/4 cup	fresh chopped parsley	60 mL
2 tbsp	dried rubbed sage	30 mL
2 tbsp	dried savory	30 mL

1. Cut loaf of bread into 1/4-inch (0.5 cm) cubes; set aside.

2. In a large microwave-safe bowl, combine celery, onions, chicken broth, parsley, sage and savory. Microwave on High for 10 minutes or until celery is tender. Pour over bread crumbs and mix well.

Variations

If you prefer, use a food processor to make coarse bread crumbs rather than making bread cubes.

Use one-third the amount of dried parsley.

Use summer savory for savory.

Baking Stuffing: Outside of the Bird

The United States Department of Agriculture (USDA), and Agriculture and Agri-Food Canada both recommend baking stuffing separately, not inside the bird.

Place stuffing in a large 16- to 20-cup (4 to 5 L) casserole dish and stir in 1/2 cup (125 mL) melted butter, pan juices or GF chicken stock. Cover and bake at 325°F (180°C) for 20 minutes after removing bird from the oven. Stuffing will bake while bird is resting before carving.

Turkey Gravy

**Makes 4 cups (1 L)
(2 tbsp/30 mL
per serving)**

When making gravy for dinner, be sure to make extra to use for hot turkey sandwiches the next day!

Tips

4 cups (1 L) gravy is enough for a 15-lb (6.8 kg) turkey.

Recipe can be doubled or tripled, but cooking time will need to be increased somewhat in each step.

Gravy thickens upon standing. When reheating, add extra liquid a little at a time until gravy reaches the desired consistency.

Gravy can be reheated either on Medium (50%) in the microwave or by simmering over medium-low heat on the stovetop.

½ cup	turkey pan drippings	125 mL
½ cup	teff flour	125 mL
3 to 4 cups	water, vegetable cooking water or GF chicken stock	750 mL to 1 L
	Salt and freshly ground black pepper	

1. When turkey is removed from the roasting pan, skim fat from pan juices. Place pan on the stovetop burners over medium heat or transfer to a saucepan, making sure to scrape all the brown bits. Sprinkle teff flour over juices. Cook, stirring constantly, for 1 minute or until gravy is the consistency of dry sand.

2. Pour in water. Bring to a boil, stirring constantly, and scraping up any brown bits from bottom of pan. Reduce heat and simmer, stirring frequently, for 5 to 10 minutes or until thickened. Add more liquid if necessary. Season to taste with salt and pepper.

Variations

Follow the same method to make beef, pork or chicken gravy.

When making gravy and sauces, substitute an equal amount of amaranth flour or sorghum flour for teff flour. This substitution cannot be made when preparing cakes, cookies, breads or pastry.

Nutrients per serving

Calories	151
Fat	5 g
Saturated fat	1 g
Cholesterol	27 mg
Sodium	333 mg
Carbohydrate	24 g
Fiber	4 g
Protein	4 g
Calcium	79 mg
Iron	2 mg

Chicken Pot Pie

Makes 6 servings

This dish is the real McCoy. We encase the chicken stew in pastry and bake it in a casserole dish. It's mm-mm delicious!

Tips

You can use fresh, canned or frozen corn.

If you prefer, use cooked meat from chicken thighs and/or legs.

- Preheat oven to 400°F (200°C)
- 8-cup (2 L) casserole dish

1 cup	baby carrots, cut in half	250 mL
2	medium potatoes, cut into ½-inch (1 cm) cubes	2
1	stalk celery, sliced	1
⅓ cup	amaranth flour	75 mL
1 cup	milk	250 mL
2 tsp	dried thyme	10 mL
4 cups	GF chicken broth	1 L
2½ lbs	cooked chicken breasts, cut into ½-inch (1 cm) cubes	1.25 kg
⅓ cup	frozen peas, thawed	75 mL
½ cup	corn kernels	125 mL
	Salt and freshly ground pepper to taste	
1	recipe Classic Pastry (page 180), unbaked	1

1. In a steamer or microwave, steam carrots, potatoes and celery just until tender. Set aside.

2. In a large saucepan, combine amaranth flour, milk, thyme and broth. Cook over medium heat, stirring constantly, until mixture boils and thickens. Add chicken, steamed vegetables, peas and corn. Season to taste with salt and pepper. Spoon stew into casserole dish.

3. Roll out pastry. Cover stew with pastry and, using a paring knife, cut steam vents. Bake in preheated oven for 25 to 35 minutes or until hot and bubbly.

Variation

Make four to six 1-cup (250 mL) individual pot pies, then freeze them. To serve, bake from frozen in preheated oven for 45 to 60 minutes or until hot and bubbly or an instant-read thermometer registers 170°F (80°C).

Nutrients per serving

Calories	812
Fat	35 g
Saturated fat	15 g
Cholesterol	209 mg
Sodium	982 mg
Carbohydrate	73 g
Fiber	6 g
Protein	49 g
Calcium	122 mg
Iron	4 mg

Chicken Fingers

Makes 4 servings

We know you will like our modern, healthier way to eat "fried" chicken! Make these gems often.

Tips

Shake off excess crumbs before baking.

Discard everything the raw chicken came in contact with, including the plastic bag — it is not safe to reuse.

- Preheat oven to 425°F (220°C)
- Rimmed baking sheet, lightly greased

4	boneless skinless chicken breasts (about 1 lb/500 g)	4
1/3 cup	sweet rice flour	75 mL
2	eggs, beaten	2
1 tbsp	water	15 mL
1 tbsp	Dijon mustard	15 mL
1 cup	fresh GF bread crumbs (see page 216)	250 mL
2/3 cup	walnuts, coarsely chopped	150 mL
1/2 cup	cornmeal	125 mL
1/4 tsp	salt	1 mL
1/4 tsp	freshly ground black pepper	1 mL

1. Pat chicken dry with paper towel. Cut each breast into 3/4-inch (2 cm) wide strips.

2. In a shallow dish or pie plate, place sweet rice flour.

3. In a second shallow dish or pie plate, whisk together eggs, water and Dijon mustard.

4. In a large plastic bag, combine bread crumbs, walnuts, cornmeal, salt and pepper.

5. Coat chicken strips, a few at a time, first in sweet rice flour, then in egg mixture. Shake in walnut–bread crumb mixture.

6. Place in a single layer 1 inch (2.5 cm) apart on prepared baking sheet. Bake in preheated oven for 20 to 25 minutes or until coating is crispy and golden brown and chicken is no longer pink inside and registers 170°F (80°C) on an instant-read thermometer.

Nutrients per serving

Calories	497
Fat	21 g
Saturated fat	2 g
Cholesterol	166 mg
Sodium	404 mg
Carbohydrate	41 g
Fiber	3 g
Protein	35 g
Calcium	46 mg
Iron	3 mg

Variations

Use boneless skinless chicken legs or thighs for part or all of the breasts.

Florentine Chicken Fingers: Top baked chicken fingers with 2 tsp (10 mL) grated Asiago cheese, 1 leaf of arugula and a strip of roasted red pepper and broil for 3 to 4 minutes, just until cheese melts.

Pizza Chicken Fingers: Top baked chicken fingers with 1 to 2 tsp (5 to 10 mL) GF pizza sauce, 2 tsp (10 mL) shredded mozzarella, and if desired, a few pieces of crumbled cooked bacon. Broil just until cheese melts.

Fish and Chips

Makes 4 servings

When Heather was growing up, fish and chips were often served as Friday night dinner. This batter is light and crisp, and it will satisfy any craving you may have for this more traditionally greasy fare. Enjoy occasionally!

Tips

Most new electric hand mixers have a wire whisk attachment, which will give you a better beating action, but a standard hand mixer works well, too.

Don't omit paprika — it helps the batter to lightly brown.

- Preheat vegetable oil in deep fryer or wok to 325°F (160°C)
- Candy/deep-fry or infrared thermometer
- Electric hand mixer fitted with wire whisk attachment (see Tips, at left)
- Fine-mesh sieve
- Baking sheets, lined with paper towel

Chips

6	large baking potatoes, peeled and cut into strips about ¼ inch (0.5 cm) thick and 3 inches (7.5 cm) long	6
1 tbsp	lemon juice	15 mL
	Salt	
	Vegetable oil for frying	

Fish

2	egg whites	2
⅓ cup	potato starch	75 mL
½ tsp	paprika	2 mL
1 lb	white fish fillets, such as sole, haddock or tilapia (each about 4 oz/125 g)	500 g
¼ cup	sweet rice flour	60 mL
	Vegetable oil for frying	

1. *Chips:* As soon as you cut the fries, place in a bowl of ice and water with lemon juice. When all fries are cut, rinse them under cold running water into bowl until water turns clear. Drain fries and dry them using a clean kitchen towel. (Adding wet potatoes to the hot oil could cause it to spatter.)

2. In prepared deep fryer or wok, cook potatoes, in batches, for 6 to 8 minutes or until soft and a slightly golden color.

3. Remove fries using a slotted spoon and transfer to prepared baking sheet to drain. Keep warm in a 300°F (150°C) oven while frying subsequent batches.

4. Heat vegetable oil until thermometer reads 375°F (190°C). Return fries, in batches, to oil and cook for another 2 to 3 minutes or until golden brown and crispy. Transfer to prepared baking sheets, then salt. Return to oven to keep warm.

5. *Fish:* Meanwhile, in a small bowl, using electric hand mixer, beat egg whites until stiff but not dry.

Nutrients per serving

Calories	557
Fat	3 g
Saturated fat	1 g
Cholesterol	51 mg
Sodium	386 mg
Carbohydrate	110 g
Fiber	8 g
Protein	24 g
Calcium	62 mg
Iron	2 mg

6. Using fine-mesh sieve, sift potato starch and paprika over beaten egg whites. Using a rubber spatula, fold it in. Set aside.

7. Rinse fish fillets under cold running water and pat dry.

8. Preheat vegetable oil again in deep fryer or wok to 350°F (180°C).

9. Dredge fish fillets in sweet rice flour. Dip into prepared egg batter to generously coat, leaving as much batter on fish as possible.

10. Deep-fry fish for 2 to 4 minutes on each side or until coating is crisp and fish is fork-tender. Transfer to a plate lined with paper towels to drain. Serve with chips.

Variations

For a spicier coating, substitute a pinch of cayenne pepper for paprika.

Use cornstarch or tapioca starch for potato starch.

Salmon Patties

**Makes 8 patties
(2 per serving)**

This is a quick evening meal that we used to make back in the day before microwaves. It's still as quick, easy and delicious today.

Tip

You can use leftover mashed potatoes in this recipe.

- Preheat oven to 450°F (230°C)
- 2 baking sheets, one lined with parchment paper, the other brushed with vegetable oil

Patties

1	medium potato, peeled and cut into quarters	1
2 tbsp	milk	30 mL
2 tsp	butter	10 mL
1	green onion, finely chopped	1
	Salt and freshly ground pepper to taste	
½ cup	chopped red bell peppers	125 mL
¼ cup	finely chopped celery	60 mL
2	eggs, beaten	2
1	tin (15½ oz/458 mL) salmon, drained, bones removed, flaked	1
	Salt and white pepper to taste	

Coating

2	eggs	2
2 cups	fine GF dry bread crumbs	500 mL

Assembly

	Lemon wedges
	Tartar sauce

1. *Patties:* In a small saucepan over high heat, bring 1 inch (2.5 cm) water to a boil. Add potato and return to a boil. Reduce heat to low and boil gently for 15 to 20 minutes or until fork-tender. Drain well.

2. Mash potato with a potato masher or fork. Add milk and butter. Stir to combine. Season to taste with salt and pepper.

3. In a bowl, combine mashed potatoes, green onion, red peppers, celery and eggs. Gently stir in salmon. Using your hands, form into 8 patties about ¾ inch (2 cm) thick.

4. *Coating:* In a pie plate or shallow dish, beat eggs.

5. Place bread crumbs in another pie plate or shallow dish.

Nutrients per serving

Calories	452
Fat	17 g
Saturated fat	3 g
Cholesterol	271 mg
Sodium	530 mg
Carbohydrate	40 g
Fiber	3 g
Protein	37 g
Calcium	70 mg
Iron	2 mg

6. Coat both sides of each patty with egg, then with bread crumbs. Place patties on prepared parchment-lined baking sheet. Discard any excess egg and bread crumbs.

7. Place oiled baking sheet in preheated oven for 5 minutes until very hot. Gently transfer patties to hot baking sheet. Bake in preheated oven for 10 minutes or until top is golden. Turn and bake for another 5 minutes or until top is golden.

8. Serve with fresh lemon wedges and tartar sauce.

Variations

Use GF cracker crumbs for GF bread crumbs.

To make cracker crumbs: Place GF crackers between two layers of waxed paper and roll with a rolling pin.

Coconut Shrimp

Makes 3 to 4 main-course servings or 6 appetizer servings

Sweet and crunchy, this popular restaurant appetizer is surprisingly easy to make — and it's great as a main course, too!

Tips

To make this recipe egg-free, substitute ½ cup (125 mL) plain yogurt or lactose-free plain yogurt for eggs.

Purchase shrimp either fresh or frozen, size 21/25 (which means in 1 lb/500 g there are 21 to 25 shrimp). Thaw frozen shrimp according to package directions before coating.

- Preheat oven to 400°F (200°C)
- Baking sheet, lightly greased

2	eggs, lightly beaten	2
1 tbsp	GF mild curry paste	15 mL
⅓ cup	cornstarch	75 mL
1 cup	unsweetened flaked coconut	250 mL
½ cup	almond flour	125 mL
24	large shrimp (about 1 lb/500 g), with tails left on, peeled and deveined	24
	GF mango chutney or cocktail or tartar sauce	

1. In a small bowl, combine eggs and curry paste.

2. In a shallow dish, place cornstarch.

3. In a separate shallow dish or pie plate, combine coconut and almond flour.

4. Holding shrimp by their tails, dip into egg mixture, coating generously. Dip into cornstarch, then back into egg mixture. Dip into coconut mixture, pressing to coat well. Arrange in a single layer on prepared baking sheet. Continue with the remaining shrimp, discarding any excess egg mixture, cornstarch and coconut mixture.

5. Bake in preheated oven for 10 to 12 minutes or until golden brown. Transfer to a serving plate and serve immediately with mango chutney.

Variations

If you like finer coconut, use shredded (smaller than flaked, but larger than grated) or grated (smallest of the three types).

Substitute coconut flour for almond flour.

Substitute amaranth flour or tapioca starch for cornstarch.

Instead of baking shrimp in a saucepan, heat 2 inches (5 cm) vegetable oil to 375°F (190°C); deep-fry 4 shrimp at a time for 1 to 2 minutes or until golden. Drain on baking sheet lined with paper towel.

Nutrients per serving

Calories	346
Fat	24 g
Saturated fat	14 g
Cholesterol	146 mg
Sodium	286 mg
Carbohydrate	19 g
Fiber	4 g
Protein	13 g
Calcium	67 mg
Iron	2 mg

Seafood Fettuccine

Makes 4 servings

This seafood pasta dish features sea scallops, shrimp and lobster meat in a cream sauce. You can also make it your own by using your favorite combination of seafood.

Tips

We used 21/25 size shrimp, which means in 1 lb (500 g) there are 21 to 25 shrimps.

1 lb (500 g) sea scallops has about 10 to 15 scallops.

Variation

Vary the seafood; substitute crabmeat for lobster meat, mussels or clams for scallops and/or add your favorite white fish.

Nutrients per serving

Calories	361
Fat	10 g
Saturated fat	6 g
Cholesterol	140 mg
Sodium	615 mg
Carbohydrate	31 g
Fiber	1 g
Protein	22 g
Calcium	152 mg
Iron	1 mg

- 12-inch (30 cm) nonstick skillet

1 cup	white wine or water	250 mL
¼ lb	fresh sea scallops	115 g
¼ lb	large frozen shrimp, defrosted, cleaned	115 g
½ lb	lobster meat	225 g
¼ lb	GF fettuccine	115 g
3 tbsp	butter	45 mL
3 tbsp	amaranth flour	45 mL
1 cup	milk	250 mL
	Salt and freshly ground pepper to taste	

1. In large skillet, heat wine over medium-low heat. Add scallops, cover and cook for 5 minutes or until firm and opaque. Drain. Set aside.

2. In a saucepan, bring 1 inch (2.5 cm) water to a simmer (almost to a boiling point, but not bubbling). Add shrimp and simmer for 3 to 5 minutes or until they have just turned pink and the tails have curled. Drain and rinse in cool water or submerge in ice water to stop the cooking process. Peel and set aside.

3. Meanwhile, in a large pot of boiling water, cook fettuccine according to package directions, until just tender. Drain well and set aside.

4. In a microwave-safe bowl, microwave butter on High for 1 to 3 minutes or until melted. Stir in amaranth flour and microwave on High for 1 to 3 minutes or until mixture is the consistency of dry sand. Stir in milk and microwave on High for 3 to 5 minutes, stirring occasionally, until mixture comes to a boil and has thickened. Season to taste with salt and pepper.

5. Transfer sauce to a large saucepan. Add cooked scallops, shrimp, lobster meat and fettuccine. Stir to combine. Warm over low heat and serve.

Quiche Lorraine

**Makes 6 pieces
(1 per serving)**

This is often our recipe of choice when having company over for lunch. Everyone enjoys this light-textured cheese, bacon and custard pie.

Tips

Refrigerate in an airtight container for up to 2 days. Serve cold, at room temperature or reheat in a 325°F (160°C) oven for 20 to 30 minutes or until warm.

¼ lb (115 g) Swiss cheese when shredded yields approximately 1 cup (250 mL).

- Preheat oven to 325°F (160°C)
- 9-inch (23 cm) deep pie plate

6 to 8	slices GF bacon, cooked crisp and crumbled	6 to 8
2	green onions (green part only), finely chopped	2
1½ cups	shredded Swiss cheese	375 mL
4	eggs, beaten	4
1½ cups	whole milk	375 mL
1 tbsp	Dijon mustard	15 mL
1	recipe Classic Pastry (page 180), baked	1

1. In a bowl, combine bacon, green onions, cheese, eggs, milk and mustard.

2. Place pie shell in pie plate on a baking sheet. Pour filling into pie shell.

3. Bake in preheated oven for 45 to 55 minutes or until a knife inserted in the middle comes out clean. Let cool on a rack for 10 minutes. Serve immediately, at room temperature or transfer to the refrigerator.

Variations

Some 9-inch (23 cm) pie plates hold more than others. If your pie plate is shallow, you might have extra filling. Bake extras in a small greased casserole dish at the same time as pie, checking occasionally for doneness. It will take between 15 and 30 minutes depending on the size and depth of casserole dish.

Make several different kinds of quiche for your next family gathering: Substitute ¼ cup (60 mL) finely diced cooked GF ham, crabmeat or shrimp for the bacon. Or add cooked broccoli or asparagus leftover from dinner the night before. Better still, cook extra especially for the quiche. You can even use an equal amount of Gruyère cheese for Swiss.

Nutrients per serving

Calories	760
Fat	52 g
Saturated fat	24 g
Cholesterol	273 mg
Sodium	712 mg
Carbohydrate	55 g
Fiber	2 g
Protein	19 g
Calcium	320 mg
Iron	2 mg

Scalloped Potatoes

Makes 4 servings

Who doesn't love scalloped potatoes? In days gone by, flour was sprinkled between the layers of potatoes, but we have updated the method for today's cooks. A cream sauce of medium thickness is made first, so there is no separation during baking.

Tip

4 cups (1 L) sliced potatoes is about 4 medium-size potatoes, and 1 lb (500 g) potatoes is 3 to 4 medium-size potatoes.

- Preheat oven to 350°F (180°C)
- 8-cup (2 L) casserole dish, lightly greased

3 tbsp	butter	45 mL
3 tbsp	amaranth flour	45 mL
¾ tsp	salt	3 mL
¼ tsp	white pepper	1 mL
1½ cups	milk	375 mL
4 cups	potatoes, peeled (optional) and thinly sliced	1 L

1. In a microwave-safe bowl, microwave butter on High for 1 to 3 minutes or until melted. Stir in amaranth flour, salt and pepper. Microwave on High for 1 to 3 minutes or until mixture is the consistency of dry sand. Stir in milk and microwave on High for 3 to 5 minutes, stirring occasionally, until mixture comes to a boil and thickens slightly.

2. In prepared casserole dish, combine potatoes and sauce.

3. Cover and bake in preheated oven for 45 minutes. Uncover and bake for 30 minutes more or until potatoes are tender and top is lightly browned. Let stand 10 minutes before serving.

Variations

Add ⅓ cup (75 mL) chopped onion when combining potatoes and sauce.

In addition to making cream sauce in microwave; cover and microwave scalloped potatoes in a microwave-safe casserole dish on Medium-High for 20 to 25 minutes or until potatoes are tender when tested with a fork. Stir twice during cooking.

Nutrients per serving

Calories	270
Fat	10 g
Saturated fat	6 g
Cholesterol	27 mg
Sodium	561 mg
Carbohydrate	40 g
Fiber	3 g
Protein	7 g
Calcium	138 mg
Iron	1 mg

Cheese Sauce for Veggies

**16 servings
(2 tbsp/30 mL each)**

Use this sauce to make macaroni and cheese or to serve over cooked vegetables. It can easily be halved or doubled.

Tips

Weight/volume equivalents for Cheddar cheese: 4 oz (125 g) = 1 cup (250 mL) shredded; 2 oz (60 g) = 1/2 cup (125 mL) shredded; 1 1/2 oz (45 g) = 1/3 cup (75 mL) shredded.

Add cheese as soon as you remove cream sauce from the microwave; otherwise, it won't all melt.

1/2 cup	shredded sharp (old) Cheddar cheese	125 mL
1/4 cup	shredded Swiss cheese	60 mL
2 tbsp	freshly grated Parmesan cheese	30 mL
2 cups	hot Medium Cream Sauce (page 91)	500 mL

1. In a small bowl, combine Cheddar, Swiss and Parmesan cheeses. Add to hot cream sauce and stir gently until cheese is melted.

Variation

Substitute Asiago, Emmental, Roquefort, Romano or any other cheeses for Cheddar, Swiss and/or Parmesan.

Nutrients per serving

Calories	68
Fat	5 g
Saturated fat	3 g
Cholesterol	15 mg
Sodium	74 mg
Carbohydrate	3 g
Fiber	0 g
Protein	3 g
Calcium	87 mg
Iron	0 mg

Cream Sauce

Makes about 1 cup (250 mL), ¼ cup (60 mL) per serving

A smooth, creamy sauce is a great starting point for many flavorful dishes. You can use the thin sauce in cream soups; the medium sauce in cheese sauce (as in page 90), vegetable sauce, casseroles and pot pie; and the thick sauce in croquettes, soufflés and puddings.

Tips

The shortest cooking time is for thin sauce; the longest is for thick.

Use a 4-cup (1 L) microwave-safe measuring cup to prepare sauce.

Cream Sauce Chart

Cream sauce	Butter	Amaranth flour	Milk
Thin	1 tbsp/15 mL	1 tbsp/15 mL	1 cup/250 mL
Medium	2 tbsp/30 mL	2 tbsp/30 mL	1 cup/250 mL
Thick	3 tbsp/45 mL	3 tbsp/45 mL	1 cup/250 mL

Add salt and freshly ground white pepper (to taste) to all of the above sauce mixtures.

1. In a microwave-safe bowl, microwave butter on High for 1 to 3 minutes or until melted. Stir in amaranth flour and microwave on High for 1 to 3 minutes or until mixture is the consistency of dry sand. Stir in milk and microwave on High for 3 to 5 minutes, stirring occasionally, until mixture comes to a boil and has thickened. Season to taste with salt and pepper.

Nutrients per serving

	Thin sauce	Medium sauce	Thick sauce
Calories	58	90	123
Fat	4 g	7 g	10 g
Saturated fat	2 g	4 g	6 g
Cholesterol	11 mg	18 mg	26 mg
Sodium	53 mg	78 mg	104 mg
Carbohydrate	4 g	6 g	7 g
Fiber	0 g	0 g	1 g
Protein	2 g	3 g	3 g
Calcium	80 mg	83 mg	86 mg
Iron	0 mg	0 mg	0 mg

Hot Cross Buns

Yeast Breads

White Bread. 96

Dinner Rolls 97

Stuffing Bread 98

Brown Sandwich Bread 100

Mock Pumpernickel Loaf. 101

Crusty French Baguette. 102

Focaccia 104

Triple-Cheese Focaccia Topping 105

Mediterranean Focaccia Topping. 106

Hot Cross Buns 108

Cinnamon Raisin Bread 110

German Christmas Stollen. 112

Raspberry Breakfast Danish 114

Tips for Stand Mixer Bread Baking Method

- Select a stand mixer with a paddle attachment for the best mixing. Gradually add dry ingredients to liquids as the machine is mixing, then stop machine and use a rubber spatula to scrape the bottom and sides of bowl. Keep in mind that the consistency of GF bread dough is more like thick cake batter than the traditional wheat dough ball.

- All 9- by 5-inch (23 by 12.5 cm) loaf pans are not the same size. We have two different types: one with straight sides and the other slightly sloped. The height of your bread can vary with the size and shape of your pan.

- Fill lightly greased pan only two-thirds full.

- Rising takes 60 to 75 minutes, but may be shorter or longer. Rising time may vary due to: the temperature of the liquids and other ingredients used in the recipe; the temperature of the room; whether there are drafts from heating or air conditioning units; the altitude and the level of humidity.

- Be patient: the loaf does most of its rising in the last 15 minutes of the rising time. Do not let it over-rise or it could collapse during baking.

- During baking, if the loaf gets as dark as desired before it is fully baked, tent it with foil for the remainder of the baking time (see the Techniques Glossary, page 218).

- Before removing the loaf from the oven, use an instant read thermometer to take the internal temperature. It should read 200°F (100°C). If it doesn't, continue baking until it does, even if the loaf looks baked. (See "Using an Instant-Read Thermometer," page 22.)

- After removing the loaf from the oven, immediately remove it from the pan and place it on a cooling rack. This will prevent a soggy loaf.

- Store bread wrapped airtight at room temperature for 1 to 2 days. Bread stored in the refrigerator dries and stales quickly. For longer storage, place 1 or 2 slices in individual plastic bags, then place those bags in a larger resealable freezer bag. Freeze for up to 3 weeks. Remove a slice or two at a time.

Tips for Bread Machine Baking Method

- Make sure your bread machine has at least one of the following choices: dedicated Gluten-Free Cycle; both a Dough Cycle and a Bake Cycle; or a Programmable Cycle. Neither the 58-minute nor the 70-minute Rapid Cycles are long enough to rise and bake loaves successfully. If you are using an older bread machine that doesn't have any of these options, try baking the loaves using a Basic or White Cycle.

- The recipes in this book were developed for 1½-lb (750 g) or 2-lb (1 kg) bread machines with either one or two kneading blades. These are the only ones you will have success with. The larger-capacity bread machines (those that bake 2½-lb/1.25 kg or 3-lb/1.5 kg loaves) are too large to properly knead the amount of dough in our recipes.

- Some machine manuals suggest warming liquids to between 110°F and 115°F (43°C and 46°C) if you're using the Gluten-Free Cycle or to between 80°F and 90°F (27°C and 32°C) if you're using the Dough Cycle. In addition, some suggest warming eggs to room temperature (see the Techniques Glossary, page 216.). Check the manual for your machine.

- The consistency of the dough is closer to a thick cake batter than the traditional wheat dough ball. The mixing mark of the kneading blade remains on top of the dough. Some doughs are thicker than others, but do not adjust by adding more liquid or dry ingredients.

- The kneading blade needs to be removed at the end of the long knead to prevent the collapse of the final loaf. However, some bread machines knead intermittently rather than continuously, so the first few times you use a new machine, listen carefully for the sounds of the different cycles. The dough is sticky, so rinse the rubber spatula and your hand with cold water before removing the blade. Smooth top of dough quickly.

- Some bread machines and some recipes bake darker-colored crusts than others. When baking on a Gluten-Free Cycle or a Basic Cycle, select a lighter crust setting, if possible.

- At the end of the baking cycle, before turning the machine off, take the temperature of the loaf using an instant-read thermometer. It should read 200°F (100°C). If it's between 180°F (85°C) and 200°F (100°C), leave the machine on the Keep Warm Cycle until the loaf is baked. If it's below 180°F (85°C), turn on the Bake Cycle and check the internal temperature every 10 minutes. (Some bread machines are automatically set for 60 minutes; others need to be set by 10-minute intervals.)

- Once the loaf has reached 200°F (100°C), immediately remove from pan and let cool completely on a rack.

White Bread

**Makes 15 slices
(1 per serving)**

This recipe has lots of
ingredients, but we find
it is worth the trouble
because the loaf slices
easily and carries well
in a packed lunch.

Tips

If you bake a lot of your own
bread, prepare extra bags of
dry ingredients to save time
when preparing the next loaf.
Store at room temperature
or freeze for longer storage,
depending on ingredients
(see page 12). Return to
room temperature before
using. Label with book page
number for easy reference.

- Stand mixer fitted with paddle attachment
- 9- by 5-inch (23 by 12.5 cm) loaf pan, lightly greased

1 cup	brown rice flour	250 mL
½ cup	amaranth flour	125 mL
⅓ cup	almond flour	75 mL
⅓ cup	quinoa flour	75 mL
⅓ cup	tapioca starch	75 mL
1 tbsp	xanthan gum	15 mL
1 tbsp	bread machine or instant yeast	15 mL
1½ tsp	salt	7 mL
2	eggs	2
1 cup	water	250 mL
2 tbsp	vegetable oil	30 mL
2 tbsp	liquid honey	30 mL
1 tsp	cider vinegar	5 mL

1. In a large bowl or plastic bag, combine brown rice flour, amaranth flour, almond flour, quinoa flour, tapioca starch, xanthan gum, yeast and salt. Mix well and set aside.

2. In mixer bowl, combine eggs, water, vegetable oil, honey and vinegar. With mixer on low speed, slowly add dry ingredients until well combined. Stop motor and scrape down the bottom and sides of bowl with a rubber spatula. With mixer on medium speed, beat for 1 minute or until smooth.

3. Spoon dough into prepared pan. Let rise, uncovered, in a warm, draft-free place for 60 to 75 minutes or until dough has risen to the top of pan.

4. Meanwhile, preheat oven to 350°F (180°C).

5. Bake for 35 to 40 minutes or until an instant-read thermometer registers 200°F (100°C). Remove from pan immediately and let cool completely on a rack.

Nutrients per serving

Calories	123
Fat	4 g
Saturated fat	1 g
Cholesterol	25 mg
Sodium	248 mg
Carbohydrate	19 g
Fiber	2 g
Protein	3 g
Calcium	17 mg
Iron	1 mg

Dinner Rolls

**Makes 12 rolls
(1 per serving)**

These white bread rolls
are great both as a dinner
accompaniment and for a
packed lunch sandwich.

Tip

Portioning with a scoop
insures all rolls are the same
size and will bake in the
same length of time.

- Stand mixer fitted with paddle attachment
- 12-cup muffin pan, lightly greased

1 cup	brown rice flour	250 mL
½ cup	amaranth flour	125 mL
⅓ cup	almond flour	75 mL
⅓ cup	quinoa flour	75 mL
⅓ cup	tapioca starch	75 mL
1 tbsp	xanthan gum	15 mL
1 tbsp	bread machine or instant yeast	15 mL
1½ tsp	salt	7 mL
2	eggs	2
1 cup	water	250 mL
2 tbsp	vegetable oil	30 mL
2 tbsp	liquid honey	30 mL
1 tsp	cider vinegar	5 mL

1. In a large bowl or plastic bag, combine brown rice flour, amaranth flour, almond flour, quinoa flour, tapioca starch, xanthan gum, yeast and salt. Mix well and set aside.

2. In mixer bowl, combine eggs, water, vegetable oil, honey and vinegar. With mixer on low speed, slowly add dry ingredients until well combined. Stop motor and scrape down the bottom and sides of bowl with a rubber spatula. With mixer on medium speed, beat for 1 minute or until smooth.

3. Using a ¼ cup (60 mL) portion scoop, divide dough into 12 equal amounts and place in cups of prepared muffin pan. Let rise, uncovered, in a warm, draft-free place for 60 to 75 minutes or until dough has risen to the top of cups.

4. Meanwhile, preheat oven to 400°F (200°C).

5. Bake for 18 to 20 minutes or until an instant-read thermometer registers 200°F (100°C). Remove from pan immediately and let cool completely on a rack.

Nutrients per serving

Calories	153
Fat	6 g
Saturated fat	1 g
Cholesterol	27 mg
Sodium	308 mg
Carbohydrate	23 g
Fiber	3 g
Protein	4 g
Calcium	20 mg
Iron	1 mg

Stuffing Bread

**Makes 15 slices
(1 per serving)**

Baking the seasonings right into the bread results in a more flavorful stuffing for your turkey.

Tips

This recipe yields 12 to 14 cups (3 to 3.5 L) stuffing.

This stuffing is perfect to enjoy with your Roast Turkey (page 72).

- Stand mixer fitted with paddle attachment
- 9- by 5-inch (23 by 12.5 cm) loaf pan, lightly greased

1 cup	brown rice flour	250 mL
½ cup	amaranth flour	125 mL
⅓ cup	almond flour	75 mL
⅓ cup	quinoa flour	75 mL
⅓ cup	tapioca starch	75 mL
¼ cup	chopped fresh parsley	60 mL
¼ cup	dried minced onion	60 mL
3 tbsp	dried rubbed sage	45 mL
3 tbsp	dried savory	45 mL
1 tbsp	xanthan gum	15 mL
1 tbsp	bread machine or instant yeast	15 mL
1½ tsp	salt	7 mL
1½ tsp	celery seeds	7 mL
2	eggs	2
1 cup	water	250 mL
2 tbsp	vegetable oil	30 mL
2 tbsp	liquid honey	30 mL
1 tsp	cider vinegar	5 mL

1. In a large bowl or plastic bag, combine brown rice flour, amaranth flour, almond flour, quinoa flour, tapioca starch, parsley, onion, sage, savory, xanthan gum, yeast, salt and celery seeds. Mix well and set aside.

2. In mixer bowl, combine eggs, water, vegetable oil, honey and vinegar. With mixer on low speed, slowly add dry ingredients until well combined. Stop motor and scrape down the bottom and sides of bowl with a rubber spatula. With mixer on medium speed, beat for 1 minute or until smooth.

3. Spoon dough into prepared pan. Let rise, uncovered, in a warm, draft-free place for 60 to 75 minutes or until dough has risen to the top of pan.

4. Meanwhile, preheat oven to 350°F (180°C).

5. Bake for 35 to 40 minutes or until an instant-read thermometer registers 200°F (100°C). Remove from pan immediately and let cool completely on a rack.

Nutrients per serving

Calories	129
Fat	5 g
Saturated fat	1 g
Cholesterol	25 mg
Sodium	249 mg
Carbohydrate	20 g
Fiber	3 g
Protein	4 g
Calcium	47 mg
Iron	2 mg

Brown Sandwich Bread

**Makes 15 slices
(1 per serving)**

For those of you who
want a rich, golden,
wholesome, nutritious
sandwich bread for
lunch, this is your loaf.

Tip
To ensure success, see
pages 94 and 95 for tips on
baking GF breads.

Variation
Add 2 tbsp (30 mL)
caraway seeds to the
dry ingredients in
Step 1.

- Stand mixer fitted with paddle attachment
- 9- by 5-inch (23 by 12.5 cm) loaf pan, lightly greased

1 cup	sorghum flour	250 mL
1/2 cup	quinoa flour	125 mL
1/3 cup	tapioca starch	75 mL
1/3 cup	rice bran	75 mL
2 tbsp	packed brown sugar	30 mL
1 tbsp	xanthan gum	15 mL
2 tsp	bread machine or instant yeast	10 mL
1 1/2 tsp	salt	7 mL
2	eggs	2
1	egg white	1
1 1/4 cups	room temperature water	300 mL
3 tbsp	vegetable oil	45 mL
2 tbsp	light (fancy) molasses	30 mL
1 tsp	cider vinegar	5 mL

1. In a large bowl or plastic bag, combine sorghum flour, quinoa flour, tapioca starch, rice bran, brown sugar, xanthan gum, yeast and salt. Mix well and set aside.

2. In mixer bowl, combine eggs, egg white, water, vegetable oil, molasses and vinegar. With mixer on low speed, slowly add dry ingredients until combined. Stop motor and scrape down the bottom and sides of bowl with a rubber spatula. With mixer on medium speed, beat for 1 minute or until smooth.

3. Spoon dough into prepared pan. Let rise, uncovered, in a warm, draft-free place for 60 to 75 minutes or until dough has risen to the top of pan.

4. Meanwhile, preheat oven to 350°F (180°C), with rack positioned in bottom third of oven.

5. Bake for 25 minutes. Tent with foil and bake for 10 to 15 minutes or until an instant-read thermometer registers 200°F (100°C). Remove from pan immediately and let cool completely on a rack.

Nutrients per serving

Calories	121
Fat	4 g
Saturated fat	1 g
Cholesterol	25 mg
Sodium	249 mg
Carbohydrate	18 g
Fiber	3 g
Protein	4 g
Calcium	14 mg
Iron	2 mg

Mock Pumpernickel Loaf

**Makes 15 slices
(1 per serving)**

This loaf has all
the hearty flavor of
traditional pumpernickel
and is great for
sandwiches. Try it filled
with sliced turkey,
accompanied by a crisp
garlic dill pickle.

Tip

Strong coffee can be
substituted for water and
instant coffee granules. Just
make sure the temperature
is not too hot or it will
inactivate the yeast.

- Stand mixer fitted with paddle attachment
- 9- by 5-inch (23 by 12.5 cm) loaf pan, lightly greased

1 cup	sorghum flour	250 mL
1/2 cup	quinoa flour	125 mL
1/3 cup	tapioca starch	75 mL
1/3 cup	rice bran	75 mL
2 tbsp	packed brown sugar	30 mL
1 tbsp	xanthan gum	15 mL
1 tbsp	instant coffee granules	15 mL
2 tsp	unsweetened cocoa powder, sifted	10 mL
2 tsp	bread machine or instant yeast	10 mL
1 1/2 tsp	salt	7 mL
1/2 tsp	ground ginger	2 mL
2	eggs	2
1	egg white	1
1 1/4 cups	room temperature water	300 mL
3 tbsp	vegetable oil	45 mL
2 tbsp	light (fancy) molasses	30 mL
1 tsp	cider vinegar	5 mL

1. In a large bowl or plastic bag, combine sorghum flour, quinoa flour, tapioca starch, rice bran, brown sugar, xanthan gum, coffee, cocoa, yeast, salt and ginger. Mix well and set aside.

2. In mixer bowl, combine eggs, egg white, water, vegetable oil, molasses and vinegar. With mixer on low speed, slowly add dry ingredients until combined. Stop motor and scrape down the bottom and sides of bowl with a rubber spatula. With mixer on medium speed, beat for 1 minute or until smooth.

3. Spoon dough into prepared pan. Let rise, uncovered, in a warm, draft-free place for 60 to 75 minutes or until dough has risen to the top of pan.

4. Meanwhile, preheat oven to 350°F (180°C), with rack positioned in bottom third of oven.

5. Bake for 25 minutes. Tent with foil and bake for 10 to 15 minutes or until an instant-read thermometer registers 200°F (100°C). Remove from pan immediately and let cool completely on a rack.

Nutrients per serving

Calories	127
Fat	4 g
Saturated fat	0 g
Cholesterol	24 mg
Sodium	250 mg
Carbohydrate	18 g
Fiber	3 g
Protein	3 g
Calcium	13 mg
Iron	2 mg

Crusty French Baguette

**Makes 12 slices
(1 per serving)**

You'll be amazed by this recipe. It's a crusty loaf with a typical French bread texture.

Tips

Store this bread, loosely covered, in a paper bag to maintain the crisp crust.

See the Equipment Glossary, page 209, for information about baguette pans.

- Stand mixer fitted with paddle attachment
- 16- x 4-inch (40 cm by 10 cm) baguette pan or baking sheet, lightly greased, lined with parchment paper and sprinkled with cornmeal

1 cup	brown rice flour	250 mL
⅓ cup	potato starch	75 mL
1 tsp	granulated sugar	5 mL
2 tsp	xanthan gum	10 mL
2 tsp	bread machine or instant yeast	10 mL
¾ tsp	salt	3 mL
1	egg white	1
¾ cup	room temperature water	175 mL
1 tsp	cider vinegar	5 mL

1. In a medium bowl or plastic bag, combine brown rice flour, potato starch, sugar, xanthan gum, yeast and salt. Set aside.

2. In mixer bowl, combine egg white, water and vinegar. With mixer on low speed, slowly add dry ingredients until combined. Stop motor and scrape the bottom and sides of bowl with a rubber spatula. With mixer on medium speed, beat for 1 minute or until smooth.

3. Spoon into one side of prepared pan or onto one half of baking sheet in the shape of a French loaf. Using the edge of a moistened rubber spatula or a sharp knife, draw three or four diagonal lines, ¼ inch (0.5 cm) deep, across top of loaf. Let rise, uncovered, in a warm, draft-free place for 60 minutes or until doubled in volume.

4. Meanwhile, preheat oven to 425°F (220°C).

5. Bake for 20 to 23 minutes or until an instant-read thermometer registers 200°F (100°C). Remove from pan immediately and let cool completely on a rack.

Variation

Garlic Cheese Bread: After Step 5, in a small bowl combine 4 crushed garlic cloves, 2 tbsp (30 mL) butter and 2 tbsp (30 mL) extra virgin olive oil in a microwave-safe dish. Microwave for 1 minute. Set aside. With a serrated knife, cutting on a diagonal, slice cooled loaf into 1-inch-thick (2.5 cm) slices. Toast under a preheated broiler for 1 to 3 minutes or until golden brown. Brush with garlic mixture and sprinkle with 2 tbsp (30 mL) grated Parmesan and ¼ cup (60 mL) chopped fresh parsley. Broil for 30 seconds to brown.

Nutrients per serving

Calories	70
Fat	0 g
Saturated fat	0 g
Cholesterol	0 mg
Sodium	153 mg
Carbohydrate	16 g
Fiber	1 g
Protein	2 g
Calcium	1 mg
Iron	0 mg

Focaccia

**Makes 4 pieces
(1 per serving)**

We enjoy focaccia
as an alternative to a
sandwich, or we cut
it into small pieces
for snacks.

Tip

Focaccia can be reheated
in just a few minutes in a
toaster oven set to 375°F
(190°C).

- Stand mixer fitted with paddle attachment
- 8-inch (20 cm) square metal baking pan, lightly
  greased and bottom lined with parchment paper

⅓ cup	amaranth flour	75 mL
¼ cup	quinoa flour	60 mL
¼ cup	tapioca starch	60 mL
1 tsp	granulated sugar	5 mL
1½ tsp	xanthan gum	7 mL
1 tbsp	bread machine or instant yeast	15 mL
½ tsp	salt	2 mL
¾ cup	room temperature water	175 mL
2 tsp	extra virgin olive oil	10 mL
1 tsp	cider vinegar	5 mL
	Topping mixtures (pages 105–106)	

1. In a medium bowl or plastic bag, combine amaranth flour, quinoa flour, tapioca starch, sugar, xanthan gum, yeast and salt. Mix well and set aside.

2. In mixer bowl, combine water, olive oil and vinegar. With mixer on low speed, slowly add dry ingredients until combined.

3. Gently transfer dough to prepared pan and using a spatula moistened with cold water, spread evenly to edges, leaving top rough and uneven. Do not smooth. Let rise, uncovered, in a warm, draft-free place for 30 minutes or until almost doubled in volume.

4. Meanwhile, preheat oven to 400°F (200°C).

5. Bake for 10 minutes or until bottom is golden. Cover with preferred topping mixture. Continue to bake for 20 to 25 minutes or until top is golden. Remove from pan immediately. Cut into four pieces and serve hot.

Nutrients per serving

Calories	126
Fat	4 g
Saturated fat	1 g
Cholesterol	0 mg
Sodium	299 mg
Carbohydrate	21 g
Fiber	4 g
Protein	3 g
Calcium	18 mg
Iron	1 mg

Triple-Cheese Focaccia Topping

Makes topping for one 8-inch (20 cm) square metal baking pan

(¼ recipe per serving)

A trio of cheeses sprinkled over focaccia dough creates the perfect bread to accompany a fresh salad.

Tip

Use the amount of cheese stated in the recipe: too much results in a greasy focaccia.

2	cloves garlic, minced	2
2 tbsp	extra virgin olive oil	30 mL
1 tbsp	dried rosemary	15 mL
1 cup	shredded Havarti cheese	250 mL
½ cup	crumbled GF blue cheese	125 mL
⅓ cup	freshly grated Parmesan cheese	75 mL
1 cup	GF salsa	250 mL

1. In a small bowl, combine garlic, olive oil and rosemary; let stand while focaccia rises and partially bakes.

2. In another small bowl, combine Havarti, blue and Parmesan cheeses; mix well and set aside.

3. Drizzle garlic-oil mixture over partially cooked focaccia. Top with cheese mixture and salsa.

Variation

Substitute your favorite lower-fat varieties for cheeses. Vary cheese mixture to suit your taste.

Nutrients per serving

Calories	385
Fat	29 g
Saturated fat	16 g
Cholesterol	59 mg
Sodium	1536 mg
Carbohydrate	9 g
Fiber	3 g
Protein	18 g
Calcium	567 mg
Iron	0 mg

Mediterranean Focaccia Topping

Makes topping for one 8-inch (20 cm) square metal baking pan

(¼ recipe per serving)

Top focaccia with sweet onions, slowly caramelized in a small amount of olive oil until golden. It's delicious for a snack or while watching a game on TV.

Tip
Take the time to caramelize onions — the flavor is worth it.

2 tbsp	extra virgin olive oil	30 mL
4 cups	sliced Vidalia or other sweet onions	1 L
2 tbsp	fresh chopped thyme	30 mL
1 tbsp	balsamic vinegar	15 mL
½ cup	dry-packed sun-dried tomatoes	125 mL
12	kalamata olives, pitted and sliced	12
½ cup	crumbled feta cheese	125 mL

1. In a skillet, heat olive oil over medium-low heat. Sauté onions for 30 minutes or until tender and light golden brown. Remove from heat and stir in thyme and vinegar. Let cool slightly.

2. Spoon over partially baked focaccia (see page 104). Sprinkle with sun-dried tomatoes, olives and feta cheese.

Variation
Substitute chopped red pepper for the sun-dried tomatoes.

Nutrients per serving

Calories	227
Fat	14 g
Saturated fat	4 g
Cholesterol	17 mg
Sodium	542 mg
Carbohydrate	22 g
Fiber	4 g
Protein	6 g
Calcium	147 mg
Iron	1 mg

Hot Cross Buns

Makes 10 buns (1 per serving)

Hot cross buns have been served on Easter since the 12th century. But before its significance for Christians, the cross symbolized the four quarters of the lunar cycle, so ancient Aztecs, Egyptians and Saxons all enjoyed hot cross buns.

Tip

Confectioners' (icing) sugar may contain up to 5% starch, which could be from wheat, so make sure to look for a GF brand.

- Stand mixer fitted with paddle attachment
- Baking sheet, lightly greased
- Fine-mesh sieve

Hot Cross Buns

¾ cup	sorghum flour	175 mL
½ cup	teff flour	125 mL
⅓ cup	tapioca starch	75 mL
1 tbsp	xanthan gum	15 mL
2 tsp	bread machine or instant yeast	10 mL
1 tsp	salt	5 mL
1½ tsp	ground cinnamon	7 mL
¼ tsp	ground cloves	1 mL
¼ tsp	ground nutmeg	1 mL
⅔ cup	milk, warmed to room temperature	150 mL
2 tbsp	vegetable oil	30 mL
1 tsp	cider vinegar	5 mL
2	eggs, lightly beaten	2
¼ cup	liquid honey	60 mL
2 tbsp	light (fancy) molasses	30 mL
1 cup	raisins	250 mL

Icing

¾ cup	GF confectioners' (icing) sugar	175 mL
1 tbsp	milk	15 mL
¼ tsp	almond extract	1 mL

1. *Hot Cross Buns:* In a large bowl or plastic bag, combine sorghum flour, teff flour, tapioca starch, xanthan gum, yeast, salt, cinnamon, cloves and nutmeg. Mix well and set aside.

2. In mixer bowl, combine milk, vegetable oil, vinegar and eggs; mix on low speed until well blended. While motor is running, slowly drizzle in honey and molasses. Slowly add dry ingredients until combined. Stop motor and scrape the bottom and sides of bowl with a rubber spatula. With mixer on medium speed, beat for 1 minute or until batter is smooth. Reduce speed to low and add raisins. Mix until combined.

Nutrients per serving

Calories	299
Fat	6 g
Saturated fat	1 g
Cholesterol	48 mg
Sodium	327 mg
Carbohydrate	60 g
Fiber	4 g
Protein	6 g
Calcium	74 mg
Iron	2 mg

3. Drop 10 heaping spoonfuls of batter onto prepared baking sheet. Using the handle of a wooden spoon or rubber spatula, make two indents $\frac{1}{8}$ inch (3 mm) deep in the shape of a cross on top of each bun. Let rise, uncovered, in a warm, draft-free place for 60 to 75 minutes or until dough has doubled in volume.

4. Meanwhile, preheat oven to 350°F (180°C).

5. Bake for 20 to 25 minutes or until an instant-read thermometer registers 200°F (100°C). Remove from pan immediately and let cool slightly on a rack.

6. *Icing:* Meanwhile, using a fine-mesh sieve, sift confectioners' sugar into a small bowl. Add milk and almond extract; mix well. Drizzle crosses of warm buns with icing.

Cinnamon Raisin Bread

**Makes 15 slices
(1 per serving)**

Enjoy a toasted slice or two of this deep golden loaf for breakfast — it's the perfect snack when served with a cup of hot cocoa.

Tip

Adding raisins with mixer on low ensures they are well combined. They will not break up during the mixing process.

Variation

For a more nutritious bread, decrease raisins to ½ cup (125 mL) and add ¼ cup (60 mL) cracked flax seeds and 2 tbsp (30 mL) millet seeds.

- **Stand mixer fitted with paddle attachment**
- **9- by 5-inch (23 by 12.5 cm) loaf pan, lightly greased**

1 cup	brown rice flour	250 mL
½ cup	amaranth flour	125 mL
⅓ cup	almond flour	75 mL
⅓ cup	quinoa flour	75 mL
⅓ cup	tapioca starch	75 mL
1 tbsp	xanthan gum	15 mL
1 tbsp	bread machine or instant yeast	15 mL
2 tsp	ground cinnamon	10 mL
1½ tsp	salt	7 mL
2	eggs	2
1 cup	water	250 mL
2 tbsp	vegetable oil	30 mL
3 tbsp	liquid honey	45 mL
1 tsp	cider vinegar	5 mL
⅔ cup	raisins	150 mL

1. In a large bowl or plastic bag, combine brown rice flour, amaranth flour, almond flour, quinoa flour, tapioca starch, xanthan gum, yeast, cinnamon and salt. Mix well and set aside.

2. In mixer bowl, combine eggs, water, vegetable oil, honey and vinegar. With mixer on low speed, slowly add dry ingredients until well combined. Stop motor and scrape down the bottom and sides of bowl with a rubber spatula. With mixer on medium speed, beat for 1 minute or until smooth. Reduce speed to low and add raisins.

3. Spoon dough into prepared pan. Let rise, uncovered, in a warm, draft-free place for 60 to 75 minutes or until dough has risen to the top of pan.

4. Meanwhile, preheat oven to 350°F (180°C).

5. Bake for 35 to 40 minutes or until an instant-read thermometer registers 200°F (100°C). Remove from pan immediately and let cool completely on a rack.

Nutrients per serving

Calories	178
Fat	4 g
Saturated fat	0 g
Cholesterol	22 mg
Sodium	250 mg
Carbohydrate	33 g
Fiber	3 g
Protein	4 g
Calcium	27 mg
Iron	1 mg

German Christmas Stollen

**Makes 16 wedges
(1 per serving)**

This is a traditional German Christmas bread with a very dark, rich-colored crust and a domed top. It is served on Christmas Eve, when families gather to celebrate before going to church.

Tips

This is a very dark loaf and must be tented to prevent the top from burning, especially any raisins that peak through the crust. Be sure to take the temperature, otherwise you are likely to think it is done before it is baked through.

Select a marmalade that is free of artificial sugars and sweeteners.

Nutrients per serving

Calories	185
Fat	4 g
Saturated fat	0 g
Cholesterol	0 mg
Sodium	175 mg
Carbohydrate	37 g
Fiber	2 g
Protein	3 g
Calcium	15 mg
Iron	1 mg

- Stand mixer fitted with paddle attachment
- 9-inch (23 cm) round metal baking pan, lightly greased
- Fine-mesh sieve

Stollen

1¼ cups	brown rice flour	300 mL
⅓ cup	quinoa flour	75 mL
¼ cup	almond flour	60 mL
⅓ cup	tapioca starch	75 mL
1 tbsp	xanthan gum	15 mL
1 tbsp	bread machine or instant yeast	15 mL
1 tsp	salt	5 mL
¾ tsp	ground cardamom	3 mL
1 cup	room temperature water	250 mL
3 tbsp	vegetable oil	45 mL
2	eggs, lightly beaten	2
½ cup	marmalade	125 mL
¾ cup	chopped mixed candied fruit	175 mL
¾ cup	raisins	175 mL

Orange Glaze

1 cup	GF confectioners' (icing) sugar	250 mL
1 to 2 tbsp	frozen orange juice concentrate, thawed	15 to 30 mL

1. *Stollen:* In a large bowl or plastic bag, combine brown rice flour, quinoa flour, almond flour, tapioca starch, xanthan gum, yeast, salt and cardamom. Mix well and set aside.

2. In mixer bowl, combine water and vegetable oil. With mixer on low speed, add eggs and marmalade. Slowly add dry ingredients until combined. Stop motor and scrape the bottom and sides of bowl with a rubber spatula. With mixer on medium speed, beat for 1 minute or until batter is smooth. Reduce speed to low and add candied fruit and raisins. Mix until combined.

3. Gently transfer dough to prepared pan, and using a spatula, smooth top so it is even to edges. Let rise, uncovered, in a warm, draft-free place for 45 minutes or until dough has risen almost to the top of pan.

4. Meanwhile, preheat oven to 350°F (180°C).

5. Bake for 40 to 45 minutes, tenting with foil after 25 minutes, until an instant-read thermometer registers 200°F (100°C). Remove from pan immediately and let cool completely on a rack.

6. *Orange glaze:* Using fine-mesh sieve, sift confectioners' sugar into a small bowl. Add enough orange juice concentrate to make a thin glaze and mix well. Drizzle over cooled stollen.

Variation
Omit orange glaze and dust with confectioners' (icing) sugar to resemble snow for a more traditional finish.

Raspberry Breakfast Danish

**Makes 6 Danish
(1 per serving)**

Every time we travel, we find Danish on the continental breakfast buffet. It's good to have a GF one that can be prepared at home.

Tips

To ensure each Danish is the same size, and they are kept at least 2 inches (5 cm) apart, take the added time to draw circles on parchment paper.

Moisten rubber spatula with cold water — you can't use too much.

Variation

Substitute applesauce for the pie filling in Danish centers.

Nutrients per serving

Calories	234
Fat	11 g
Saturated fat	1 g
Cholesterol	31 mg
Sodium	409 mg
Carbohydrate	31 g
Fiber	4 g
Protein	6 g
Calcium	46 mg
Iron	2 mg

- Bread machine
- Baking sheet, lightly greased, lined with parchment paper

Danish

¾ cup	amaranth flour	175 mL
½ cup	almond flour	125 mL
½ cup	tapioca starch	125 mL
¼ cup	granulated sugar	60 mL
2 tsp	xanthan gum	10 mL
1 tbsp	bread machine or instant yeast	15 mL
1 tsp	salt	5 mL
½ cup	room temperature water	125 mL
2 tbsp	vegetable oil	30 mL
1 tsp	cider vinegar	5 mL
1	egg, lightly beaten	1

Filling

1	package (8 oz/250 g) light or regular brick cream cheese, softened	1
½ cup	granulated sugar	125 mL
½ cup	raspberry jam	125 mL

1. *Danish:* In a large bowl or plastic bag, combine amaranth flour, almond flour, tapioca starch, sugar, xanthan gum, yeast and salt. Mix well and set aside.

2. Pour water, vegetable oil and vinegar into bread machine baking pan. Add eggs. Select dough cycle. As bread machine is mixing, gradually add dry ingredients, scraping bottom and sides of pan with a rubber spatula. Try to incorporate all dry ingredients within 1 to 2 minutes. Stop bread machine as soon as the kneading portion of the cycle is complete. Do not let bread machine finish the cycle.

3. Meanwhile, draw six 4½-inch (11 cm) circles on parchment paper at least 2 inches (5 cm) apart onto prepared baking sheet. Using a ⅓-cup (75 mL) portion scoop, place a scoop of dough on each. Using a moistened rubber spatula, spread each scoop to fill circle. Let rise, uncovered, in a warm, draft-free place for 60 minutes or until doubled in volume.

4. Meanwhile, preheat oven to 350°F (180°C).

5. *Filling:* In a small bowl, beat together cream cheese and sugar. Spread a generous 2 tbsp (30 mL) filling on top of each dough circle and spoon 2 tsp (10 mL) jam in the center.

6. Bake in preheated oven for 15 to 20 minutes or until edges are lightly browned. Remove from pan immediately and let cool completely on a rack.

Date Nut Loaf

Yeast-Free Muffins and Biscuits

Banana Chocolate Chip Muffins 120

Carrot Raisin Muffins 122

Mock Date Bran Muffins .123

Banana Bread 124

Date Nut Loaf 126

Basic Rich Biscuits 127

Strawberry Shortcake. 128

Cheese Biscuits Two Ways 130

Cornbread. 132

Buttermilk Scones 134

Irish Soda Bread 136

Baking Tips for Quick Breads and Muffins

- The batters should be the same consistency as wheat flour batters. It is not possible to overmix gluten-free muffin batters.

- Use a portion scoop to quickly divide the batter into prepared muffin cups to ensure muffins are equal in size and bake in the same length of time.

- The size of the muffin changes the baking time. Mini muffins take 12 to 15 minutes to bake, while jumbo muffins bake in 20 to 40 minutes. Check jumbo muffins for doneness after 20 minutes, then again every 5 minutes. Keep in mind that the baking time will vary with the amount of batter in each muffin cup.

- Fill muffin pans and loaf pans no more than three-quarters full.

- Let batter-filled pans stand for 30 minutes before baking for a more tender product. It's worth the wait. We set a timer for 20 minutes, then preheat the oven so both the oven and the batter are ready at the same time.

- If muffins stick to the lightly greased pans, let stand for a minute or two and try again. Loosen with a spatula, if necessary.

- To freeze, place individual muffins or loaf slices in small freezer bags, then place them all in a large freezer bag. Freeze for up to 1 month.

Baking Tips for Biscuits and Scones

- When cutting cold butter into the dry ingredients, keep in mind that the task goes more quickly when the butter is precut into 1-inch (2.5 cm) cubes. We sometimes grate the cold butter instead. Cold butter results in light, fluffy biscuits. Use it directly out of the refrigerator.

- To make drop biscuits, spoon the dough onto a large serving spoon and push it off onto the baking sheet with the back of another spoon.

- Biscuits should all be the same size to bake in the same length of time.

- Biscuits are baked when they are golden on both top and bottom. Immediately remove them from baking sheets or the bottoms may become soggy.

- Make only a few biscuits at a time. They are at their best served warm from the oven.

- To reheat leftover biscuits, wrap loosely in a paper towel and microwave each biscuit on Medium for a few seconds.

Banana Chocolate Chip Muffins

**Makes 12 muffins
(1 per serving)**

This is definitely a recipe for breakfast, lunch or a snack. It combines two of our favorite flavors for all ages to enjoy.

Tip

Measure the banana exactly. It will take about 3 bananas, but don't add more than 1¼ cups (300 mL).

- Electric hand mixer
- 12-cup muffin pan, lightly greased

1 cup	sorghum flour	250 mL
½ cup	brown rice flour	125 mL
¼ cup	tapioca starch	60 mL
¼ cup	packed brown sugar	60 mL
1½ tsp	xanthan gum	7 mL
2 tsp	GF baking powder	10 mL
1 tsp	baking soda	5 mL
¼ tsp	salt	1 mL
2	eggs	2
1¼ cups	mashed banana	300 mL
3 tbsp	vegetable oil	45 mL
1 tsp	freshly squeezed lemon juice	5 mL
¾ cup	semisweet chocolate chips	175 mL

1. In a large bowl or plastic bag, combine sorghum flour, brown rice flour, tapioca starch, brown sugar, xanthan gum, baking powder, baking soda and salt. Mix well and set aside.

2. In a separate bowl, using electric hand mixer, beat eggs, banana, vegetable oil and lemon juice until combined. Add dry ingredients and mix until just combined. Stir in chocolate chips.

3. Spoon batter evenly into prepared muffin cups. Let stand for 30 minutes.

4. Meanwhile, preheat oven to 350°F (180°C).

5. Bake for 22 to 24 minutes or until firm to the touch. Remove from pan immediately and let cool completely on a rack.

Variation

To make a loaf, spoon batter into a lightly greased 9- by 5-inch (23 by 12.5 cm) metal loaf pan. Let stand for 30 minutes. Meanwhile, preheat oven to 350°F (180°C). Bake for 55 to 65 minutes or until a tester inserted in the center comes out clean. Let cool in pan on a rack for 10 minutes. Remove from pan and let cool completely on rack.

Nutrients per serving

Calories	227
Fat	9 g
Saturated fat	3 g
Cholesterol	31 mg
Sodium	169 mg
Carbohydrate	36 g
Fiber	3 g
Protein	4 g
Calcium	51 mg
Iron	1 mg

Carrot Raisin Muffins

**Makes 12 muffins
(1 per serving)**

Enjoy carrot cake, but
don't want a large cake?
Try this muffin recipe.

Tip

Shred carrots just before
using; exposure to air causes
them to darken.

Variation

Substitute quinoa flour
for whole bean flour.

- Electric hand mixer
- 12-cup muffin pan, lightly greased

1¼ cups	sorghum flour	300 mL
⅓ cup	whole bean flour	75 mL
¼ cup	tapioca starch	60 mL
1½ tsp	xanthan gum	7 mL
1 tbsp	GF baking powder	15 mL
½ tsp	baking soda	2 mL
½ tsp	salt	2 mL
¾ tsp	ground allspice	3 mL
2	eggs	2
1½ cups	shredded carrots	375 mL
2 tbsp	grated orange zest	30 mL
¾ cup	freshly squeezed orange juice	175 mL
⅓ cup	liquid honey	75 mL
¼ cup	vegetable oil	60 mL
1 cup	raisins	250 mL

1. In a large bowl or plastic bag, combine sorghum flour, whole bean flour, tapioca starch, xanthan gum, baking powder, baking soda, salt and allspice. Mix well and set aside.

2. In a separate bowl, using electric hand mixer, beat eggs, carrots, orange zest, orange juice, honey and vegetable oil until combined. Add dry ingredients and mix until just combined. Stir in raisins.

3. Spoon batter evenly into prepared muffin cups. Let stand for 30 minutes.

4. Meanwhile, preheat oven to 350°F (180°C).

5. Bake for 18 to 20 minutes or until firm to the touch. Remove from pan immediately and let cool completely on a rack.

Nutrients per serving

Calories	204
Fat	6 g
Saturated fat	1 g
Cholesterol	31 mg
Sodium	175 mg
Carbohydrate	36 g
Fiber	3 g
Protein	4 g
Calcium	79 mg
Iron	1 mg

Mock Date Bran Muffins

**Makes 12 muffins
(1 per serving)**

These muffins are rich, dark and tasty — they travel well, too.

Tip
See the baking tips on page 118 before trying this recipe.

Variations
For a milder flavored bran muffin, substitute an equal amount of liquid honey for half the molasses.

Substitute GF rice bran for GF oat bran.

- Electric hand mixer
- 12-cup muffin pan, lightly greased

1 cup	sorghum flour	250 mL
⅔ cup	whole bean flour	150 mL
¼ cup	tapioca starch	60 mL
¼ cup	GF oat bran	60 mL
¼ cup	packed brown sugar	60 mL
1 tbsp	GF baking powder	15 mL
1 tsp	baking soda	5 mL
1½ tsp	xanthan gum	7 mL
½ tsp	salt	2 mL
2	eggs	2
1½ cups	buttermilk	375 mL
¼ cup	vegetable oil	60 mL
¼ cup	light (fancy) molasses	60 mL
¾ cup	chopped dates	175 mL

1. In a bowl or plastic bag, combine sorghum flour, whole bean flour, tapioca starch, oat bran, brown sugar, baking powder, baking soda, xanthan gum and salt. Mix well and set aside.

2. In a separate bowl, using electric mixer, beat eggs, buttermilk, vegetable oil and molasses until combined. Add dry ingredients and mix just until combined. Stir in dates.

3. Spoon batter evenly into prepared muffin cups. Let stand for 30 minutes.

4. Meanwhile, preheat oven to 350°F (180°C).

5. Bake for 19 to 22 minutes or until firm to the touch. Remove from pan immediately and let cool completely on a rack.

Nutrients per serving

Calories	212
Fat	7 g
Saturated fat	1 g
Cholesterol	33 mg
Sodium	247 mg
Carbohydrate	35 g
Fiber	4 g
Protein	6 g
Calcium	134 mg
Iron	2 mg

Banana Bread

**Makes 12 slices
(1 slice per serving)**

This is the go-to recipe when your bananas are ripening faster than you want.

Tip
You'll need about 3 very ripe bananas for 1½ cups (375 mL) mashed. Do not add extra.

Variation
Add ½ cup (125 mL) chopped walnuts or pecans to dry ingredients in Step 2.

- Electric hand mixer
- 9- by 5-inch (23 by 12.5 cm) loaf pan, lightly greased

1½ cups	mashed bananas	375 mL
¼ cup	milk	60 mL
1 tsp	cider vinegar	5 mL
1 cup	sorghum flour	250 mL
⅔ cup	teff flour	150 mL
¼ cup	tapioca starch	60 mL
⅓ cup	packed brown sugar	75 mL
1 tbsp	GF baking powder	15 mL
½ tsp	baking soda	2 mL
1½ tsp	xanthan gum	7 mL
¼ tsp	salt	1 mL
1	egg, lightly beaten	1
¼ cup	vegetable oil	60 mL

1. In a large bowl, combine bananas, milk and vinegar. Let stand for 5 minutes.

2. In a bowl or plastic bag, combine sorghum flour, teff flour, tapioca starch, brown sugar, baking powder, baking soda, xanthan gum and salt. Mix well and set aside.

3. Add egg and vegetable oil to banana mixture. Using electric hand mixer, beat until combined. Add dry ingredients and mix just until combined.

4. Spoon batter into prepared pan. Let stand for 30 minutes.

5. Meanwhile, preheat oven to 350°F (180°C).

6. Bake for 55 to 65 minutes or until a tester inserted in the center comes out clean. Let cool in pan on a rack for 10 minutes. Remove from pan and let cool completely on rack.

Nutrients per serving

Calories	173
Fat	6 g
Saturated fat	1 g
Cholesterol	16 mg
Sodium	114 mg
Carbohydrate	29 g
Fiber	3 g
Protein	3 g
Calcium	81 mg
Iron	1 mg

Date Nut Loaf

**Makes 12 slices
(1 per serving)**

Serve this loaf when a
friend visits for morning
coffee or afternoon tea.
It travels well, too.

Tip

If you purchase chopped
dates instead of whole dates,
be sure to check for gluten.

Variation

Date Nut Muffins:
Spoon batter evenly
into each cup of a
prepared 12-cup muffin
pan. Let stand for
30 minutes. Meanwhile,
preheat oven to 350°F
(180°C). Bake for 18 to
20 minutes or until firm
to the touch. Remove
from pan immediately
and let cool completely
on a rack.

Nutrients per serving

Calories	240
Fat	8 g
Saturated fat	1 g
Cholesterol	31 mg
Sodium	322 mg
Carbohydrate	40 g
Fiber	4 g
Protein	5 g
Calcium	25 mg
Iron	1 mg

- **Electric hand mixer**
- **9- by 5-inch (23 by 12.5 cm) loaf pan, lightly greased**

1¼ cups	coarsely chopped dates	300 mL
½ cup	chopped walnuts	125 mL
3 tbsp	vegetable oil	45 mL
2 tsp	baking soda	10 mL
½ tsp	salt	2 mL
1 cup	boiling water	250 mL
¾ cup	sorghum flour	175 mL
⅔ cup	amaranth flour	150 mL
¼ cup	tapioca starch	60 mL
¾ cup	granulated sugar	175 mL
1½ tsp	xanthan gum	7 mL
2	eggs	2
1 tsp	vanilla extract	5 mL

1. In a medium bowl, combine dates, walnuts, vegetable oil, baking soda and salt. Pour in boiling water and set aside for 20 minutes.

2. In a large bowl or plastic bag, combine sorghum flour, amaranth flour, tapioca starch, sugar and xanthan gum. Mix well and set aside.

3. In a separate bowl, using electric hand mixer, beat eggs and vanilla until combined. Stir in date mixture. Add dry ingredients and mix just until combined.

4. Spoon batter into prepared loaf pan. Let stand for 30 minutes.

5. Meanwhile, preheat oven to 350°F (180°C).

6. Bake for 55 to 65 minutes or until a tester inserted in the center comes out clean. Let cool in pan on a rack for 10 minutes. Remove from pan and let cool completely on rack.

Basic Rich Biscuits

**Makes 8 biscuits
(1 per serving)**

These are quick and easy
to make while dinner
is cooking. Serve with
Chicken Fingers (page 78)
and fresh broccoli.

Tips

To drop dough from a spoon,
scoop it onto a large serving
spoon and push it off onto
baking sheet with back of
another spoon.

Biscuits should all be
the same size to bake
in the same length of time.

Variation

For an herb biscuit,
add ¼ cup (60 mL)
fresh parsley and
1½ tsp (7 mL) fresh dill,
rosemary, marjoram
or savory.

- Preheat oven to 400°F (200°C)
- Baking sheet, lightly greased

⅔ cup	milk	150 mL
1 tsp	cider vinegar	5 mL
⅔ cup	brown rice flour	150 mL
½ cup	sorghum flour	125 mL
¼ cup	tapioca starch	60 mL
1 tbsp	granulated sugar	15 mL
2 tbsp	GF baking powder	30 mL
1 tsp	baking soda	5 mL
1½ tsp	xanthan gum	7 mL
¼ tsp	salt	1 mL
½ cup	cold butter, cut into ½-inch (1 cm) cubes	125 mL

1. In a measuring cup or small bowl, combine milk and vinegar. Set aside for 5 minutes.

2. In a large bowl, combine brown rice flour, sorghum flour, tapioca starch, sugar, baking powder, baking soda, xanthan gum and salt.

3. Using a pastry blender or two knives, cut in butter until mixture resembles coarse crumbs about the size of small peas. Add milk mixture all at once, stirring with a fork to make a sticky dough.

4. Drop dough by heaping spoonfuls 2 inches (5 cm) apart on prepared baking sheet. Bake in preheated oven for 13 to 15 minutes or until tops are golden. Serve immediately.

Nutrients per serving

Calories	211
Fat	12 g
Saturated fat	8 g
Cholesterol	32 mg
Sodium	345 mg
Carbohydrate	24 g
Fiber	2 g
Protein	3 g
Calcium	193 mg
Iron	1 mg

Strawberry Shortcake

**Makes 5 biscuits
(1 per serving)**

One of our favorite seasons begins when pick-your-own strawberries are available. Serve for afternoon tea or invite neighbors for lunch in your garden.

Tips

Cold butter cuts more easily into dry ingredients than soft butter and produces flakier biscuits. For easier handling, first cut butter into 1-inch (2.5 cm) cubes.

We love using a biscuit base for our shortcakes, but you could use wedges of White Cake (page 175) or Sponge Cake (page 174) if you prefer.

- Preheat oven to 425°F (220°C)
- English muffin rings (see Equipment Glossary, page 209), lightly greased, placed on a lightly greased baking sheet

1 cup	brown rice flour	250 mL
1/3 cup	almond flour	75 mL
1/3 cup	tapioca starch	75 mL
3 tbsp	granulated sugar	45 mL
1 tsp	xanthan gum	5 mL
1 tbsp	GF baking powder	15 mL
1/2 tsp	baking soda	2 mL
1 tsp	grated lemon zest	5 mL
1/2 tsp	salt	2 mL
1/3 cup	cold butter, cut into 1-inch (2.5 cm) cubes (see Tip, at left)	75 mL
1 cup	plain yogurt	250 mL
1 quart	strawberries, sliced	1 L
	Whipped cream	

1. In a large bowl, stir together brown rice flour, almond flour, tapioca starch, sugar, xanthan gum, baking powder, baking soda, lemon zest and salt.

2. Using a pastry blender or two knives, cut in butter until mixture resembles coarse crumbs. Add yogurt, all at once, stirring with a fork to make a soft, sticky dough.

3. Spoon dough into rings. Bake in preheated oven for 12 to 15 minutes or until tops are golden. Remove to a cooling rack immediately. Remove from rings.

4. Cut biscuits in half horizontally. Fill and top with sliced fresh strawberries. Serve with a dollop of whipped cream.

Variation

If you do not have English muffin rings, biscuits can be dropped by large spoonfuls onto a lightly greased baking sheet to create 8 large drop biscuits.

Nutrients per serving

Calories	396
Fat	18 g
Saturated fat	9 g
Cholesterol	36 mg
Sodium	512 mg
Carbohydrate	57 g
Fiber	5 g
Protein	8 g
Calcium	261 mg
Iron	2 mg

Cheese Biscuits Two Ways

**Makes 8 biscuits
(1 per serving)**

Who doesn't love cheese biscuits? We dare you to try and eat just one!

- Preheat oven to 425°F (220°C)
- Baking sheet

Food Processor Method

- Food processor

¾ cup	almond flour	175 mL
¾ cup	brown rice flour	175 mL
2 tbsp	granulated sugar	30 mL
1 tbsp	GF baking powder	15 mL
1 tsp	baking soda	5 mL
1 tsp	xanthan gum	5 mL
¼ tsp	salt	1 mL
⅛ tsp	dry mustard	0.5 mL
¼ cup	cold butter, cut into 1-inch (2.5 cm) cubes	60 mL
¼ cup	freshly grated Parmesan cheese	60 mL
¼ cup	grated sharp (old) Cheddar cheese	60 mL
¾ cup	GF sour cream	175 mL

1. In food processor fitted with metal blade, pulse almond flour, brown rice flour, sugar, baking powder, baking soda, xanthan gum, salt and dry mustard. Add butter, Parmesan and Cheddar cheeses, and pulse until mixture resembles small peas, for 5 to 10 seconds. Add sour cream all at once and pulse 3 or 4 times until dough just holds together. Do not overprocess.

2. Drop dough by heaping spoonfuls 2 inches (5 cm) apart on baking sheet.

3 Bake in preheated oven for 13 to 15 minutes or until tops are golden. Serve immediately.

Nutrients per serving

Calories	237
Fat	17 g
Saturated fat	7 g
Cholesterol	30 mg
Sodium	364 mg
Carbohydrate	19 g
Fiber	2 g
Protein	6 g
Calcium	178 mg
Iron	1 mg

Tip

Our favorite Tex Mex cheese mix contains Cheddar, mozzarella and Monterey Jack cheeses with jalapeño peppers. We buy it grated, so it's easy to substitute.

Traditional Method

¾ cup	almond flour	175 mL
¾ cup	brown rice flour	175 mL
2 tbsp	granulated sugar	30 mL
1 tbsp	GF baking powder	15 mL
1 tsp	baking soda	5 mL
1 tsp	xanthan gum	5 mL
¼ tsp	salt	1 mL
⅛ tsp	dry mustard	0.5 mL
¼ cup	cold butter, cut into 1-inch (2.5 cm) cubes	60 mL
¼ cup	freshly grated Parmesan cheese	60 mL
¼ cup	grated sharp (old) Cheddar cheese	60 mL
¾ cup	GF sour cream	175 mL

1. In a large bowl, combine almond flour, brown rice flour, sugar, baking powder, baking soda, xanthan gum, salt and dry mustard. Using a pastry blender or two knives, cut in butter until mixture resembles coarse crumbs. Stir in Parmesan and Cheddar cheeses. Add sour cream all at once, stirring with a fork to make a soft, sticky dough.

2. Drop dough by heaping spoonfuls 2 inches (5 cm) apart on baking sheet.

3. Bake in preheated oven for 13 to 15 minutes or until tops are golden. Serve immediately.

Variations

To make a bacon cheese biscuit, add 6 slices GF bacon, cooked crisp and crumbled, with dry ingredients in Step 1. Make sure to drain bacon on a plate lined with paper towels.

Substitute GF blue cheese or Swiss cheese for the Cheddar.

For an onion cheese biscuit, add ½ cup (125 mL) finely chopped green onions (about 6 in total).

Cornbread

Makes 8 pieces (1 per serving)

This is a favorite in Texas with beanless chili or in Ontario with black bean chili. No one can resist a slice of warm cornbread.

Tips

If you don't have buttermilk on hand, add 1 tsp (5 mL) lemon juice or vinegar to 1 cup (250 mL) milk and let stand for 5 to 10 minutes.

Butter works best in this recipe. Do not substitute a low-calorie margarine.

- Preheat oven to 375°F (190°C)
- 8-inch (20 cm) round metal baking pan, lightly greased

¾ cup	cornmeal	175 mL
⅔ cup	brown rice flour	150 mL
⅓ cup	amaranth flour	75 mL
2 tbsp	tapioca starch	30 mL
2 tbsp	granulated sugar	30 mL
2 tsp	xanthan gum	10 mL
2 tsp	GF baking powder	10 mL
1 tsp	baking soda	5 mL
½ tsp	salt	2 mL
1 cup	buttermilk	250 mL
½ cup	butter, melted and cooled	125 mL

1. In a large bowl, combine cornmeal, brown rice flour, amaranth flour, tapioca starch, sugar, xanthan gum, baking powder, baking soda and salt. Set aside.

2. In a medium bowl, combine buttermilk and butter. Add to cornbread mixture all at once, stirring with a fork to make a slightly sticky dough.

3. Spoon dough into prepared pan, leaving top rough.

4. Bake in preheated oven for 20 to 25 minutes or until top is golden. Serve immediately.

Variation

Bacon Cheddar Cornbread: Add 4 to 6 slices GF bacon, cooked crisp and crumbled, and ½ cup (125 mL) shredded sharp (old) Cheddar cheese to dry ingredients in Step 1.

Broccoli Cheese Cornbread: Add ½ cup (125 mL) shredded Havarti or Asiago cheese in Step 1. Fold in ⅓ cup (75 mL) corn niblets and ½ cup (125 mL) broccoli florets at the end of Step 2.

Nutrients per serving

Calories	259
Fat	13 g
Saturated fat	8 g
Cholesterol	33 mg
Sodium	436 mg
Carbohydrate	33 g
Fiber	2 g
Protein	4 g
Calcium	109 mg
Iron	1 mg

Buttermilk Scones

**Makes 6 wedges
(1 per serving)**

This recipe reminds us
of the southern states,
where scones are served
hot for breakfast, instead
of toast.

Tips

If you don't have buttermilk
on hand, substitute plain
yogurt or GF sour cream.

Choose white teff flour for
a lighter colored scone.

- Preheat oven to 350°F (180°C)
- 8-inch (20 cm) round metal baking pan, lightly greased
  and bottom lined with parchment paper

Food Processor Method

- Mini food processor

2	egg yolks	2
½ cup	buttermilk	125 mL
⅔ cup	teff flour	150 mL
¼ cup	amaranth flour	60 mL
2 tbsp	tapioca starch	30 mL
2 tbsp	granulated sugar	30 mL
1 tbsp	GF baking powder	15 mL
1 tsp	baking soda	5 mL
1 tsp	xanthan gum	5 mL
⅛ tsp	salt	0.5 mL
3 tbsp	cold butter, cut into 1-inch (2.5 cm) cubes	45 mL

1. In a measuring cup or small bowl, whisk together egg yolks
   and buttermilk. Set aside.

2. In mini food processor fitted with metal blade, combine teff
   flour, amaranth flour, tapioca starch, sugar, baking powder,
   baking soda, xanthan gum and salt; pulse 3 to 5 times to
   combine. Add butter and pulse for 6 to 10 seconds or until
   mixture resembles coarse crumbs about the size of small
   peas. Add egg yolk mixture all at once and process just
   until dough holds together.

3. Spoon dough into prepared pan, leaving top rough. Bake
   in preheated oven for 24 to 28 minutes or until top is deep
   golden. Cut into wedges and serve immediately.

Nutrients per serving

Calories	177
Fat	8 g
Saturated fat	5 g
Cholesterol	78 mg
Sodium	335 mg
Carbohydrate	22 g
Fiber	3 g
Protein	4 g
Calcium	175 mg
Iron	2 mg

Traditional Method

2	egg yolks	2
½ cup	buttermilk	125 mL
⅔ cup	teff flour	150 mL
¼ cup	amaranth flour	60 mL
2 tbsp	tapioca starch	30 mL
2 tbsp	granulated sugar	30 mL
1 tbsp	GF baking powder	15 mL
1 tsp	baking soda	5 mL
1 tsp	xanthan gum	5 mL
⅛ tsp	salt	0.5 mL
3 tbsp	cold butter, cut into 1-inch (2.5 cm) cubes	45 mL

1. In a measuring cup or small bowl, whisk together egg yolks and buttermilk. Set aside.

2. In a bowl, combine teff flour, amaranth flour, tapioca starch, sugar, baking powder, baking soda, xanthan gum and salt. Using a pastry blender or two knives, cut in butter until mixture resembles coarse crumbs about the size of small peas. Add egg yolk mixture all at once, stirring with a fork to make a thick dough.

3. Spoon dough into prepared pan, leaving top rough. Bake in preheated oven for 24 to 28 minutes or until top is deep golden. Cut into wedges and serve immediately.

Irish Soda Bread

**Makes 8 wedges
(1 per serving)**

This quick-to-prepare
bread is perfect if you
have eliminated yeast
from your diet. Serve
with an Irish stew.

Tip

To make almond flour, see
the Techniques Glossary,
page 217.

- Preheat oven to 375°F (190°C)
- 8-inch (20 cm) round metal baking pan, lightly greased

1 cup	milk	250 mL
1 tsp	freshly squeezed lemon juice	5 mL
⅔ cup	brown rice flour	150 mL
½ cup	almond flour	125 mL
¼ cup	quinoa flour	60 mL
¼ cup	tapioca starch	60 mL
2 tbsp	granulated sugar	30 mL
1½ tsp	xanthan gum	7 mL
1½ tsp	baking soda	7 mL
1 tsp	cream of tartar	5 mL
¼ tsp	salt	1 mL
¼ cup	cold butter, cut into ½-inch (1 cm) cubes	60 mL

1. In a measuring cup or bowl, combine milk and lemon juice. Set aside for 5 minutes.

2. In a large bowl, combine brown rice flour, almond flour, quinoa flour, tapioca starch, sugar, xanthan gum, baking soda, cream of tartar and salt. Using a pastry blender or two knives, cut in butter until mixture resembles coarse crumbs about the size of small peas. Add milk mixture all at once, stirring with a fork to make a soft, slightly sticky dough.

3. Spoon dough into prepared pan. With a sharp knife, lightly score eight ⅛-inch-deep (3 mm) wedges. Bake in preheated oven for 20 to 25 minutes or until a tester inserted in the center comes out clean. Let cool in pan on a rack for 10 minutes. Cut into wedges and serve warm.

Variation

Add 1 cup (250 mL) raisins, currants and/or chopped walnuts to dry ingredients in Step 2 before adding milk mixture.

Nutrients per serving

Calories	193
Fat	10 g
Saturated fat	4 g
Cholesterol	17 mg
Sodium	378 mg
Carbohydrate	23 g
Fiber	2 g
Protein	4 g
Calcium	58 mg
Iron	1 mg

Oatmeal Raisin Cookies and
Cherry Almond Biscotti (variation)

Cookies, Bars and Squares

Almond Biscotti 142

Oatmeal Raisin Cookies. 143

Ginger Snaps 144

Shortbread Cookies. 146

Chocolate Chip Cookies 147

Peanut Butter Chunk Cookies. 148

Nanaimo Bars 150

Date Squares 151

Lemon Squares. 152

Fudgy Brownies 154

Baking Tips for Cookies, Bars and Squares

- Using granulated sugar, rather than either brown sugar or honey, generally results in crisper cookies. Equal amounts may be substituted one for the other.

- Using butter, rather than shortening, in a cookie usually causes the dough to spread more during baking, creating a flatter, crisper cookie. You can substitute one for the other or use part of each in a recipe to get the texture you want. Do not use a diet, low-fat or buttery spread. When creaming the butter, beat just until smooth but not airy.

- Bake a test cookie to check the accuracy of your oven's temperature setting. You may need to increase or reduce the temperature slightly or adjust the baking time. This is a good time to check the consistency of the dough. If the dough is too soft, it will spread during baking, and the resultant cookie will be too thin. Add 1 to 2 tbsp (15 to 30 mL) sweet rice flour if necessary.

- When making cutout cookies, roll out the dough between two layers of waxed paper or parchment paper. If the dough becomes too soft and sticky, refrigerate for 15 minutes. Roll out the dough to a uniform thickness for more even baking. Use as little sweet rice flour as possible when rerolling dough. Cut out shapes as close together as possible.

- Shiny baking sheets produce soft-bottomed cookies, while darker pans result in crisper cookies.

- When baking two sheets at once, place them in the upper and lower thirds of the oven. Switch their positions halfway through the suggested baking time.

- When baking with only one baking sheet, let it cool for 2 or 3 minutes between batches.

- During baking, keep your eyes on the oven, not the clock — 1 to 2 minutes can mean the difference between undercooked and burnt cookies.

- Let baked cookies cool on the baking sheet on a rack for 1 to 2 minutes, then remove from the baking sheet and place, without overlapping, on the rack to cool completely.

- Store moist, soft cookies and crisp, hard cookies separately. Soft cookies should be stored layered between sheets of waxed paper in an airtight container, so they stay soft and moist. Crisp cookies should be lightly wrapped in a covered but not airtight container.

- Freeze cookies, squares and bars in an airtight container between sheets of waxed paper for up to 2 months.

- Store dough wrapped airtight in the refrigerator for up to 5 days or in the freezer for up to 2 months. Thaw in the refrigerator overnight. Bring to room temperature before baking.

- When making cookies, prepare enough dough for about 4 to 6 dozen. Bake 1 or 2 dozen, and form the remaining dough into logs. Each log should have enough dough to make 1 or 2 dozen cookies. Wrap the logs airtight and freeze. There is no need to thaw the dough completely. Let a log thaw just enough to be able to slice it into $\frac{1}{2}$-inch (1 cm) circles. You'll be able to bake cookies without having to prepare the dough from scratch each time.

Almond Biscotti

**Makes 24 cookies
(1 per serving)**

Biscotti, a traditional Italian cookie, has become part of North American cuisine. We like to dip them in hot coffee.

Tips

Cut dough, with a sharp knife, into the exact number of slices specified in the recipe, so they bake in the allotted time.

For information on toasting nuts, see the Techniques Glossary (page 217).

- Preheat oven to 325°F (160°C)
- Electric hand mixer
- 8-inch (20 cm) square metal baking pan, lightly greased

¾ cup	amaranth flour	175 mL
¼ cup	almond flour	60 mL
2 tbsp	tapioca starch	30 mL
2 tbsp	cornstarch	30 mL
¾ tsp	xanthan gum	3 mL
½ tsp	GF baking powder	2 mL
¼ tsp	salt	1 mL
2	eggs	2
⅓ cup	granulated sugar	75 mL
½ tsp	almond extract	2 mL
¾ cup	sliced almonds, toasted	175 mL

1. In a large bowl or plastic bag, combine amaranth flour, almond flour, tapioca starch, cornstarch, xanthan gum, baking powder and salt. Mix well and set aside.

2. In a separate bowl, using electric hand mixer, beat eggs, sugar and almond extract until combined. Slowly beat in dry ingredients until just combined. Stir in almonds.

3. Spoon into prepared pan. Using a moistened rubber spatula, spread batter to edges and smooth top.

4. Bake in preheated oven for 30 to 35 minutes or until firm and top is just turning golden. Let cool in pan for 5 minutes. Remove from pan and let cool on a cutting board for 5 minutes. Cut into quarters, then cut each quarter into 6 slices.

5. Arrange slices upright (both cut-sides exposed) at least ½ inch (1 cm) apart on baking sheet(s). Bake for 15 minutes until dry and crisp. Transfer baking sheet(s) to a rack and let cool completely. Store in an airtight container at room temperature for up to 3 weeks or freeze for up to 2 months.

Variations

Substitute hazelnuts and hazelnut flour for almonds and almond flour.

Add ½ cup (125 mL) dried sour cherries or dried cranberries with almonds in Step 2.

Nutrients per serving

Calories	59
Fat	3 g
Saturated fat	0 g
Cholesterol	16 mg
Sodium	32 mg
Carbohydrate	7 g
Fiber	1 g
Protein	2 g
Calcium	22 mg
Iron	1 mg

Oatmeal Raisin Cookies

**Makes 48 cookies
(1 per serving)**

Now that pure GF oats
are available, you are
able to enjoy this
traditional cookie.

Tips

The combination of brown
and white sugar gives
the cookies a texture that
resembles more traditional
oatmeal cookies.

Underbake by a minute or
two for a chewy cookie.
Bake longer for a crisper one.
Watch carefully, as cookies
burn within an extra 1 to
2 minutes.

- Preheat oven to 350°F (180°C)
- Electric hand mixer
- 1 or 2 baking sheets, lightly greased

¾ cup	GF oat flour	175 mL
¼ cup	tapioca starch	60 mL
½ tsp	xanthan gum	2 mL
¾ tsp	baking soda	3 mL
¾ cup	butter, softened	175 mL
½ cup	granulated sugar	125 mL
½ cup	packed brown sugar	125 mL
1	egg	1
2 tsp	vanilla extract	10 mL
2½ cups	GF large-flake (old-fashioned) oats	625 mL
1½ cups	raisins	375 mL

1. In a small bowl or plastic bag, combine oat flour, tapioca starch, xanthan gum and baking soda. Mix well and set aside.

2. In a large bowl, using electric hand mixer, cream butter. Add sugar, brown sugar, egg and vanilla, and beat until light and fluffy. Slowly stir in dry ingredients until combined. Stir in oats and raisins.

3. Drop dough by rounded spoonfuls 2 inches (5 cm) apart on prepared baking sheet(s). Bake in preheated oven for 10 to 13 minutes or until lightly browned and just set. Let cool on baking sheet(s) on a rack for 2 to 3 minutes. Carefully transfer cookies to rack and let cool completely. Store in an airtight container at room temperature for up to 5 days or freeze for up to 2 months.

Variations

For a chewier cookie, replace white sugar with packed brown sugar.

Brown rice flour can replace GF oat flour, but the flavor and texture may be slightly gritty.

Nutrients per serving

Calories	96
Fat	4 g
Saturated fat	2 g
Cholesterol	12 mg
Sodium	48 mg
Carbohydrate	15 g
Fiber	1 g
Protein	2 g
Calcium	11 mg
Iron	1 mg

Ginger Snaps

**Makes 36 cookies
(1 per serving)**

Donna traditionally serves these cookies at Christmas but enjoy them anytime.

Tips

If the dough sticks to the cookie cutter, dip cutter in a saucer of sorghum flour or return dough to the refrigerator until thoroughly chilled.

Watch cookies carefully while baking: a couple of extra minutes can cause them to burn on the bottom.

Variation

For a more crinkled look, roll dough into balls, then into 2 to 3 tbsp (30 to 45 mL) of sugar before flattening.

Nutrients per serving

Calories	78
Fat	3 g
Saturated fat	2 g
Cholesterol	12 mg
Sodium	70 mg
Carbohydrate	12 g
Fiber	1 g
Protein	1 g
Calcium	16 mg
Iron	1 mg

- Electric hand mixer
- 2-inch (5 cm) cookie cutter
- 2 baking sheets, lightly greased

1½ cups	sorghum flour	375 mL
⅔ cup	whole bean flour	150 mL
⅓ cup	tapioca starch	75 mL
1 tsp	xanthan gum	5 mL
¾ tsp	baking soda	3 mL
¼ tsp	salt	1 mL
1½ tsp	ground ginger	7 mL
1 tsp	ground cinnamon	5 mL
½ tsp	ground cloves	2 mL
½ cup	butter, softened	125 mL
⅓ cup	packed brown sugar	75 mL
½ cup	light (fancy) molasses	125 mL
2 tsp	finely grated gingerroot	10 mL
1 tbsp	cider vinegar	15 mL
1	egg	1

1. In a large bowl or plastic bag, combine sorghum flour, whole bean flour, tapioca starch, xanthan gum, baking soda, salt, ginger, cinnamon and cloves. Mix well and set aside.

2. In a separate large bowl, using electric hand mixer, cream butter, brown sugar, molasses, gingerroot, vinegar and egg. Slowly beat in dry ingredients until just combined. Divide dough into thirds. Wrap each in plastic wrap. Flatten slightly into a disc and refrigerate overnight.

3. Preheat oven to 350°F (180°C).

4. Remove one disc of dough from the refrigerator. Discard plastic wrap. Place on a sheet of parchment paper and cover with another sheet of parchment paper. Roll out to just under ¼ inch (0.5 cm) thick. Cut out circles with cookie cutter, rerolling scraps as necessary. Repeat with the remaining dough.

5. Place cookies 1 inch (2.5 cm) apart on prepared baking sheets. Bake one sheet at a time in top third of oven for 10 to 12 minutes or until tops crack slightly. Let cool on baking sheets on racks for 1 minute. Transfer cookies to racks and let cool completely. Store in an airtight container at room temperature for up to 5 days or in the freezer for up to 2 months.

Shortbread Cookies

**Makes 8 wedges
(1 wedge per serving)**

These shortbread triangles are made in large traditional rounds, then cut into wedges. Handle with care — they are very fragile.

Tip
Sprinkle tops with a little superfine sugar while cookies are still warm from the oven.

- Preheat oven to 300°F (150°C)
- Electric hand mixer
- Baking sheet, lined with parchment paper

⅓ cup	brown rice flour	75 mL
3 tbsp	cornstarch	45 mL
3 tbsp	potato starch	45 mL
⅓ cup	sifted GF confectioners' (icing) sugar	75 mL
½ tsp	xanthan gum	2 mL
⅓ cup	butter, softened	75 mL
1½ tsp	almond extract	7 mL

1. Using a pencil, draw a 5-inch (12.5 cm) circle on parchment paper–lined baking sheet.

2. In a bowl or plastic bag, combine brown rice flour, cornstarch, potato starch, confectioners' sugar and xanthan gum. Mix well and set aside.

3. In a separate bowl, using electric hand mixer, cream butter and almond extract. Gradually beat in dry ingredients just until combined. With a rubber spatula, scrape bottom and sides of bowl.

4. Gather dough into a large ball, kneading in any remaining dry ingredients. Form into a disc and place in center of circle, cover with parchment and roll out dough to fit circle. Remove parchment. Using a sharp knife, cut through almost to bottom of dough, into 8 wedges. Prick all over with a fork.

5. Bake in preheated oven for 33 to 37 minutes or until set and lightly browned around edges. Let cool completely on baking sheet on a rack. Store in an airtight container at room temperature for up to 2 weeks or in the freezer for up to 2 months.

Variation
Roll dough into 1-inch (2.5 cm) balls. Place 2 inches (5 cm) apart on baking sheet lined with parchment paper and flatten with a fork dipped in sweet rice flour. Bake for 15 to 20 minutes or until set and lightly browned around edges. Let cool on baking sheet on rack for 2 minutes. Transfer cookies to rack and let cool completely.

Nutrients per serving

Calories	140
Fat	8 g
Saturated fat	5 g
Cholesterol	20 mg
Sodium	69 mg
Carbohydrate	17 g
Fiber	1 g
Protein	1 g
Calcium	3 mg
Iron	0 mg

Chocolate Chip Cookies

**Makes 36 cookies
(1 per serving)**

These classic cookies
are everyone's favorite.

Tip
Don't stack freshly baked
cookies on a plate — spread
them out on a rack to cool.

- Preheat oven to 350°F (180°C)
- Electric hand mixer
- 1 or 2 baking sheets, lightly greased

1 cup	sorghum flour	250 mL
¾ cup	whole bean flour	175 mL
⅓ cup	tapioca starch	75 mL
¼ tsp	xanthan gum	1 mL
½ tsp	baking soda	2 mL
⅓ cup	butter, softened	75 mL
⅓ cup	shortening, softened	75 mL
⅔ cup	packed brown sugar	150 mL
3	eggs	3
1 tsp	vanilla extract	5 mL
1½ cups	chocolate chips	375 mL
⅔ cup	chopped walnuts	150 mL

1. In a large bowl or plastic bag, combine sorghum flour, whole bean flour, tapioca starch, xanthan gum and baking soda. Mix well and set aside.

2. In a separate bowl, using electric hand mixer, cream butter and shortening. Add brown sugar, eggs and vanilla until well blended. Slowly beat in dry ingredients just until combined. Stir in chocolate chips and walnuts.

3. Drop dough by rounded spoonfuls 2 inches (5 cm) apart on prepared baking sheet(s). Bake in preheated oven for 10 to 12 minutes or until set. Let cool on baking sheet(s) on a rack for 2 minutes. Transfer cookies to rack and let cool completely.

Variations
For a crisper cookie, substitute an equal amount of butter for shortening.

Substitute white chocolate chips for chocolate chips and macadamia nuts for walnuts.

Nutrients per serving

Calories	128
Fat	8 g
Saturated fat	3 g
Cholesterol	20 mg
Sodium	41 mg
Carbohydrate	14 g
Fiber	1 g
Protein	2 g
Calcium	13 mg
Iron	1 mg

Peanut Butter Chunk Cookies

**Makes 36 cookies
(1 per serving)**

These were Donna's
younger son's favorite
cookies when he was
growing up. He called
them "round roads
cookies." He still asks
for them.

Tip

If the dough sticks to the
fork while flattening, dip fork
into sweet rice flour.

Variation

For a crisper cookie,
shortening can be
substituted for butter.

- Preheat oven to 350°F (180°C)
- Electric hand mixer
- 1 or 2 baking sheets, lightly greased

1 cup	amaranth flour	250 mL
¼ cup	quinoa flour	60 mL
¼ cup	cornstarch	60 mL
½ tsp	xanthan gum	2 mL
½ tsp	baking soda	2 mL
¼ tsp	salt	1 mL
¼ cup	butter, softened	60 mL
1 cup	chunky peanut butter	250 mL
1 cup	packed brown sugar	250 mL
½ tsp	vanilla extract	2 mL
1	egg	1
½ cup	unsalted peanuts, coarsely chopped	125 mL

1. In a large bowl or plastic bag, combine amaranth flour, quinoa flour, cornstarch, xanthan gum, baking soda and salt. Mix well and set aside.

2. In a separate bowl, using electric hand mixer, cream butter, peanut butter and brown sugar. Add vanilla and egg; beat until well blended. Slowly beat in dry ingredients and peanuts until combined.

3. Roll dough into 1-inch (2.5 cm) balls. Place 2 inches (5 cm) apart on prepared baking sheet(s). Flatten slightly with a fork.

4. Bake in preheated oven for 10 to 12 minutes or until set. Let cool on baking sheet(s) on a rack for 2 minutes. Transfer cookies to rack and let cool completely. Store in an airtight container at room temperature for up to 5 days or freeze for up to 2 months.

Nutrients per serving

Calories	110
Fat	6 g
Saturated fat	2 g
Cholesterol	9 mg
Sodium	84 mg
Carbohydrate	12 g
Fiber	1 g
Protein	3 g
Calcium	15 mg
Iron	1 mg

Nanaimo Bars

**Makes 24 bars
(1 per serving)**

We could not develop recipes for a classics cookbook without including this recipe for our Canadian friends, although we know those south of the border will enjoy them, too. They are named after the city on Vancouver Island, British Columbia.

Tips

One individually wrapped square of baking chocolate equals 1 oz (30 g).

If custard powder is not available, substitute commercial Lemon Jell-O powder.

- Electric hand mixer
- 8-inch (20 cm) square metal pan, lightly greased and bottom lined with parchment

Base

1	egg	1
1 tsp	almond extract	5 mL
⅓ cup	butter, melted and cooled	75 mL
⅓ cup	unsweetened cocoa powder, sifted	75 mL
2 tbsp	granulated sugar	30 mL
2 cups	hazelnut flour	500 mL
1 cup	unsweetened desiccated coconut	250 mL
½ cup	chopped hazelnuts	125 mL

Filling

¼ cup	butter	60 mL
3 tbsp	milk	45 mL
¼ cup	custard powder	60 mL
2 cups	sifted confectioners' (icing) sugar	500 mL

Glaze

1 tbsp	butter	15 mL
3 oz	semisweet chocolate, cut into 6 pieces	90 g

1. *Base:* In a large bowl, blend together egg and almond extract. Add butter, cocoa, sugar, hazelnut flour, coconut and hazelnuts. Stir until combined. Spread evenly in prepared pan. Chill completely.

2. *Filling:* In a separate bowl, using electric hand mixer, cream butter. Slowly add milk, custard powder and confectioners' sugar. Mix until combined. Spread over base and chill in the refrigerator for 30 to 45 minutes.

3. *Glaze:* In a small bowl, microwave butter and chocolate on Medium for 1 to 2 minutes. Stir until completely melted. Drizzle over chilled filling. Refrigerate for at least 1 hour before cutting into squares.

Variations

Substitute white cake crumbs, almond flour or pecan flour for hazelnut flour.

Substitute pecans for hazelnuts and pecan flour for hazelnut flour.

Nutrients per serving

Calories	216
Fat	16 g
Saturated fat	6 g
Cholesterol	21 mg
Sodium	6 mg
Carbohydrate	19 g
Fiber	2 g
Protein	3 g
Calcium	25 mg
Iron	1 mg

Date Squares

**Makes 16 squares
(1 per serving)**

These squares are very
attractive on a plate of
cookies. They disappear
fast, so bake extra and
store in the freezer.

Tips

For information about GF
oat flakes and GF oat flour,
see page 9.

The recipe can easily be
doubled and baked in a
13- by 9-inch (33 by 23 cm)
metal baking pan for 40 to
45 minutes.

A 12 oz/375 g package of
dates yields 2 cups (500 mL).

- Preheat oven to 350°F (180°C)
- 8-inch (20 cm) square metal baking pan, lightly greased

¾ cup	water	175 mL
1¼ cups	snipped dates	300 mL
1⅓ cups	GF large-flake (old-fashioned) oats	325 mL
⅔ cup	amaranth flour	150 mL
⅔ cup	GF oat flour	150 mL
⅔ cup	granulated sugar	150 mL
¼ tsp	salt	1 mL
½ cup	butter, melted	125 mL

1. In a medium saucepan, combine water and dates. Bring to a boil over medium heat. Reduce heat to low and simmer uncovered, stirring often, for about 8 minutes or until mixture resembles the consistency of jam. Remove from heat and let cool slightly.

2. In a large bowl, combine oats, amaranth flour, oat flour, sugar and salt. Stir in melted butter until mixture is soft and crumbly.

3. Reserve 1½ cups (375 mL) of crumb mixture for topping. Firmly pat the remaining mixture into prepared pan. Spread cooked date mixture evenly over base and sprinkle with reserved crumb mixture. Do not press mixture down; it should be crumbly on top.

4. Bake in preheated oven for 30 to 35 minutes or until light golden brown. Let cool completely in pan on a rack. Cut into squares. Store in an airtight container in the refrigerator for up to 5 days or freeze for up to 2 months.

Nutrients per serving

Calories	197
Fat	7 g
Saturated fat	4 g
Cholesterol	15 mg
Sodium	89 mg
Carbohydrate	31 g
Fiber	3 g
Protein	3 g
Calcium	22 mg
Iron	1 mg

Variations

If you are unable to tolerate oats, substitute buckwheat, quinoa or amaranth flakes for GF large-flake (old-fashioned) oats and sorghum flour for GF oat flour.

Squares are delicious served warm for dessert. If serving as a dessert, cut into 9 larger squares.

Lemon Squares

**Makes 36 squares
(1 per serving)**

This tangy citrus treat
is a favorite — a true
classic loved by all.

Tip

If your baking pan has a
light-colored finish, bake
base for an extra 3 minutes
and topping for up to an
extra 5 minutes. Light
reflects heat, whereas a
dark finish absorbs it.

Variation

While the squares are
still warm, dust with
GF confectioners'
(icing) sugar. Cut into
larger pieces and serve
with strawberries or
raspberries for dessert.

- Preheat oven to 350°F (180°C)
- Food processor
- 9-inch (23 cm) square metal baking pan, lightly
  greased and bottom lined with parchment paper
- Electric hand mixer

Base

¼ cup	amaranth flour	60 mL
¾ cup	cornstarch	175 mL
3 tbsp	tapioca starch	45 mL
1 tsp	xanthan gum	5 mL
¼ cup	packed brown sugar	60 mL
Pinch	salt	Pinch
⅓ cup	vegetable oil	75 mL
1	egg	1

Topping

4	eggs	4
1½ cups	granulated sugar	375 mL
2 tbsp	grated lemon zest	30 mL
½ cup	freshly squeezed lemon juice	125 mL
¼ cup	cornstarch	60 mL
1 tsp	GF baking powder	5 mL

1. *Base:* In food processor fitted with metal blade, pulse
   amaranth flour, cornstarch, tapioca starch, xanthan gum,
   brown sugar and salt to combine. In a small bowl, whisk
   vegetable oil and egg. With motor running, add egg
   mixture in a slow, steady stream through feed tube and
   process for 5 to 10 seconds or until mixture resembles
   coarse crumbs.

2. Press evenly into bottom of prepared pan. Bake in
   preheated oven for 12 to 15 minutes or until set.

3. Reduce oven temperature to 325°F (160°C).

4. *Topping:* Meanwhile, in a bowl, using electric hand mixer,
   beat eggs, sugar, lemon zest, lemon juice, cornstarch and
   baking powder until blended. Pour over hot base.

5. Bake for 35 to 40 minutes or until light golden and firm
   to the touch. Let cool completely in pan on a rack, then
   cut into squares.

Nutrients per serving

Calories	86
Fat	3 g
Saturated fat	0 g
Cholesterol	26 mg
Sodium	11 mg
Carbohydrate	15 g
Fiber	0 g
Protein	1 g
Calcium	13 mg
Iron	0 mg

Fudgy Brownies

Makes 16 servings

Brownies prepared with a combination of semisweet and unsweetened chocolate have an interesting depth of flavor. You will enjoy this unique taste.

Tip

See the Techniques Glossary (page 216) for information about melting chocolate.

Variation

It's easy to double the recipe: use a 13- x 9-inch (33 by 23 cm) metal baking pan and bake for 40 to 45 minutes.

- Preheat oven to 325°F (160°C)
- Electric hand mixer
- 8-inch (20 cm) square metal baking pan, lightly greased and bottom lined with parchment

⅓ cup	low-fat soy or teff flour	75 mL
2 tbsp	tapioca starch	30 mL
1 tsp	xanthan gum	5 mL
1 tsp	GF baking powder	5 mL
½ cup	butter	125 mL
1 cup	granulated sugar	250 mL
1 tsp	vanilla extract	5 mL
2	eggs	2
2	1 oz/30 g squares unsweetened chocolate, melted and cooled slightly	2
2	1 oz/30 squares semisweet chocolate, melted and cooled slightly	2
½ cup	chopped walnuts	125 mL

1. In a medium bowl or plastic bag, combine soy flour, tapioca starch, xanthan gum and baking powder. Mix well and set aside.

2. In a large bowl, using electric hand mixer, cream butter, sugar and vanilla. Beat in eggs until light and fluffy. Stir in chocolate. Stir in dry ingredients and walnuts.

3. Spoon batter into prepared pan and spread to edges with a moistened rubber spatula. Bake 30 to 35 minutes or until a tester inserted in the middle comes out slightly moist. Let cool completely in pan on a rack.

Nutrients per serving

Calories	181
Fat	12 g
Saturated fat	6 g
Cholesterol	39 mg
Sodium	62 mg
Carbohydrate	18 g
Fiber	2 g
Protein	4 g
Calcium	30 mg
Iron	1 mg

Red Velvet Cake with Red Velvet Frosting

Cakes

Almond Pound Cake 159

Frosted Carrot Cake. 160

Cottage Pudding with Brown Sugar Sauce 162

Fruitcake 164

Blueberry Hazelnut Crumble Coffee Cake 166

Raspberry Jelly Roll 168

German Chocolate Cake. 170

Red Velvet Cake 172

Cream Cheese Frosting. 173

Red Velvet Frosting 173

Sponge Cake 174

White Cake 175

Cake-Baking Tips

- We always use metal pans in recipes. If you use an ovenproof glass pan, reduce the temperature by 25°F (5°C).

- We recommend sifting individual gluten-free flours and starches before measuring, then mixing well when combining because gluten-free flours and starches clump easily. Without thorough mixing, the resultant cake may bake with pockets of these ingredients.

- In cake recipes, the butter or shortening is often creamed with the sugar before the eggs are added. Your cake or cupcakes will have a better texture if you cream the butter first, then gradually beat in the sugar. Then add the eggs, one at a time, beating after each, for the lightest possible cake.

- To lighten baked foods containing eggs, we like to separate the eggs and beat the whites until stiff but not dry, then fold them into the batter as the last step before spooning the batter into the baking pan.

- Letting the batter stand for 30 minutes at room temperature before baking results in lighter-textured, more tender cakes. But if you're short on time, you can bake immediately.

- Test the cakes for doneness: the top of the cake should spring back when pressed lightly; a tester inserted in the center should come out clean; and the internal temperature should reach 200°F (100°C).

- Unless the recipe specifies otherwise, let cakes cool in the pan for 10 minutes. Then run a metal spatula or knife between the pan and the cake and turn the cake out onto a cooling rack. Let cool completely before frosting.

- You can freeze unfrosted cakes, wrapped airtight, for up to 6 weeks. Thaw in the refrigerator for several hours or overnight. Frost after the cake thaws.

Almond Pound Cake

Makes 9 servings

This cake has a more compact texture than a layer cake. We enjoy it with an afternoon cup of tea or coffee.

Tips

Let cake cool completely, then wrap it tightly and freeze for up to 6 weeks. Thaw wrapped cake in the refrigerator for several hours or overnight.

See the Techniques Glossary (page 217) for more information about toasting almonds.

Variation

Substitute milk for almond milk.

Nutrients per serving

Calories	281
Fat	16 g
Saturated fat	2 g
Cholesterol	62 mg
Sodium	309 mg
Carbohydrate	29 g
Fiber	3 g
Protein	7 g
Calcium	112 mg
Iron	1 mg

- Electric hand mixer
- 8-inch (20 cm) square metal baking pan, lightly greased and bottom lined with parchment paper

²⁄₃ cup	almond flour	150 mL
¹⁄₃ cup	brown rice flour	75 mL
¹⁄₄ cup	amaranth flour	60 mL
¹⁄₄ cup	tapioca starch	60 mL
2 tsp	xanthan gum	10 mL
2 tsp	GF baking powder	10 mL
1 tsp	baking soda	5 mL
¹⁄₂ tsp	salt	2 mL
3	eggs	3
²⁄₃ cup	granulated sugar	150 mL
¹⁄₂ cup	unsweetened almond milk	125 mL
¹⁄₄ cup	vegetable oil	60 mL
1¹⁄₂ tsp	almond extract	7 mL
²⁄₃ cup	slivered almonds, lightly toasted	150 mL

1. In a large bowl or plastic bag, combine almond flour, brown rice flour, amaranth flour, tapioca starch, xanthan gum, baking powder, baking soda and salt. Mix well and set aside.

2. In a separate bowl, using electric hand mixer, beat eggs, sugar, almond milk, vegetable oil and almond extract until combined. Add dry ingredients and almonds, and mix until just combined.

3. Spoon batter into prepared pan. Using a moistened rubber spatula, spread batter to edges and smooth top. Let stand for 30 minutes.

4. Meanwhile, preheat oven to 350°F (180°C).

5. Bake for 30 to 35 minutes or until a tester inserted in the center comes out clean. Let cool in pan on a rack for 10 minutes. Remove from pan and let cool completely on rack.

Frosted Carrot Cake

Makes
12 to 16 servings

A popular choice for a birthday cake. Everyone at the party will enjoy this special treat.

Tips
Moistening the rubber spatula with cold water makes it easier to spread the thick cake batter evenly into the corners.

You can use light or regular cream cheese in this recipe. "Spreadable" or "whipped" cream cheese cannot be used because it is too soft to set the icing.

Variation
Substitute an equal amount of raisins for walnuts or add half of each.

Nutrients per serving

Calories	236
Fat	7 g
Saturated fat	2 g
Cholesterol	40 mg
Sodium	190 mg
Carbohydrate	40 g
Fiber	3 g
Protein	5 g
Calcium	81 mg
Iron	2 mg

- Electric hand mixer
- 13- by 9-inch (33 by 23 cm) metal baking pan, lightly greased and bottom lined with parchment paper

Carrot Cake

1¼ cups	brown rice flour	300 mL
1 cup	amaranth flour	250 mL
¼ cup	quinoa flour	60 mL
¼ cup	tapioca starch	60 mL
2 tsp	xanthan gum	10 mL
2 tsp	GF baking powder	10 mL
1 tsp	baking soda	5 mL
½ tsp	salt	2 mL
1½ tsp	ground cinnamon	7 mL
½ tsp	ground nutmeg	2 mL
3	eggs	3
1¼ cups	packed brown sugar	300 mL
¾ cup	sour cream	175 mL
1 cup	crushed pineapple, including juice	250 mL
2 cups	shredded carrots	500 mL
¾ cup	chopped walnuts	175 mL
1	recipe Cream Cheese Frosting (page 173)	1

1. *Carrot Cake:* In a large bowl or plastic bag, combine brown rice flour, amaranth flour, quinoa flour, tapioca starch, xanthan gum, baking powder, baking soda, salt, cinnamon and nutmeg.

2. In a separate bowl, using electric hand mixer, beat eggs, brown sugar, sour cream and pineapple until well blended. Gradually beat in dry ingredients. Stir in carrots and walnuts.

3. Spoon batter into prepared pan. Using a moistened rubber spatula, spread batter to edges and smooth top. Let stand for 30 minutes.

4. Meanwhile, preheat oven to 350°F (180°C).

5. Bake for 40 to 50 minutes or until a tester inserted in the center comes out clean.

6. Remove cake from oven. Let cool in pan on a rack for 10 minutes. Remove from pan and let cool completely on rack. Spread cream cheese frosting on the top and sides of cake.

Cottage Pudding with Brown Sugar Sauce

Makes 8 servings

Donna always has this cake in the freezer in case company drops in. It only takes a few minutes to make the brown sugar sauce.

Tip

To freeze for later use: Make sure to let cake cool completely. Cut cake into 8 pieces, then tightly wrap each individually. Place in a labeled freezer bag and freeze cake for up to 6 weeks. Individual pieces thaw quickly and will be ready by the time you prepare the sauce.

Nutrients per serving

Calories	344
Fat	16 g
Saturated fat	3 g
Cholesterol	78 mg
Sodium	253 mg
Carbohydrate	46 g
Fiber	2 g
Protein	6 g
Calcium	91 mg
Iron	1 mg

- Electric hand mixer
- 8-inch (20 cm) square metal baking pan, lightly greased and bottom lined with parchment paper

Cottage Pudding

½ cup	almond flour	125 mL
½ cup	brown rice flour	125 mL
¼ cup	amaranth flour	60 mL
¼ cup	potato starch	60 mL
1½ tsp	xanthan gum	7 mL
2 tsp	GF baking powder	10 mL
1 tsp	baking soda	5 mL
½ tsp	salt	2 mL
3	eggs	3
½ cup	granulated sugar	125 mL
½ cup	milk	125 mL
¼ cup	vegetable oil	60 mL
1 tsp	almond extract	5 mL

Brown Sugar Sauce

½ cup	packed brown sugar	125 mL
2 tbsp	cornstarch	30 mL
⅛ tsp	salt	0.5 mL
1¼ cups	water	300 mL
2 tbsp	butter	30 mL
1 tsp	vanilla	5 mL

1. *Cottage Pudding:* In a large bowl or plastic bag, combine almond flour, brown rice flour, amaranth flour, potato starch, xanthan gum, baking powder, baking soda and salt. Mix well and set aside.

2. In a separate bowl, using electric hand mixer, beat eggs, sugar, milk, vegetable oil and almond extract until combined. Add dry ingredients and mix until just combined.

3. Spoon batter into prepared pan. Using a moistened rubber spatula, spread batter to edges and smooth top. Let stand for 30 minutes.

4. Meanwhile, preheat oven to 350°F (180°C).

You can also serve brown sugar sauce over ice cream. Leftover sauce can be refrigerated for 1 week or frozen for up to 4 weeks.

5. Bake for 30 to 35 minutes or until a tester inserted in the center comes out clean. Let cool in pan on a rack for 10 minutes. Remove from pan and let cool on rack.

6. *Brown Sugar Sauce:* In a medium saucepan, combine brown sugar, cornstarch and salt. Slowly add water, stirring constantly. Bring to a boil over medium-high heat, stirring constantly. Boil for 2 to 3 minutes or until thick and shiny. Remove from heat. Stir in butter and vanilla.

7. Cut cake into 8 pieces. Top each piece with sauce. Serve warm.

Variations
Rather than serving with sauce, frost cooled cake with your favorite chocolate icing.

To turn brown sugar sauce into hot brandy sauce, add 2 tbsp (30 mL) brandy with butter in Step 6.

Fruitcake

**Makes 2 cakes
20 pieces each
(1 piece per serving)**

What would Christmas be without fruitcake? Our recipe falls somewhere between the traditional light and dark versions. We like to make two at a time, so that we can give one away as a gift and keep one for ourselves.

- Two 9- by 5-inch (23 by 12.5 cm) loaf pans
- Shallow 13- by 9-inch (33 by 23 cm) metal baking pan
- Stand mixer fitted with paddle attachment

3 cups	mixed candied peel	750 mL
2 cups	sultana raisins	500 mL
1½ cups	green and red glacé cherries, halved	375 mL
1 cup	candied pineapple, coarsely chopped	250 mL
¾ cup	slivered almonds	175 mL
½ cup	unsweetened apple juice	125 mL
1 cup	sorghum flour	250 mL
½ cup	almond flour	125 mL
⅓ cup	tapioca starch	75 mL
2 tsp	xanthan gum	10 mL
1 tsp	baking soda	5 mL
¼ tsp	salt	1 mL
⅓ cup	butter, softened	75 mL
⅔ cup	granulated sugar	150 mL
2	eggs	2
⅔ cup	crushed pineapple, including juice	150 mL
1 tsp	almond extract	5 mL

1. In a large bowl, combine peel, raisins, cherries, candied pineapple, almonds and apple juice; cover and let stand for 8 hours or overnight, stirring 2 or 3 times.

2. Line bottom and sides of each loaf pan with a double layer of lightly greased heavy brown paper and one layer of parchment paper.

3. Position two oven racks to divide oven into thirds. Fill baking pan with at least 1 inch (2.5 cm) hot water and place on bottom shelf. Preheat oven to 275°F (140°C).

4. In a large bowl or plastic bag, combine sorghum flour, almond flour, tapioca starch, xanthan gum, baking soda and salt. Mix well and set aside.

5. In mixer bowl, combine butter and sugar; with mixer on high speed, cream until light and fluffy. Add eggs, one at a time, beating well after each addition. Reduce speed to low and add crushed pineapple and almond extract. Gradually add dry ingredients until smooth. Stir in fruit mixture.

Nutrients per serving

Calories	343
Fat	7 g
Saturated fat	2 g
Cholesterol	27 mg
Sodium	186 mg
Carbohydrate	72 g
Fiber	4 g
Protein	4 g
Calcium	70 mg
Iron	1 mg

6. Spoon batter evenly into prepared loaf pans. Using a moistened rubber spatula, spread batter to edges and smooth tops.

7. Bake cakes on top rack of oven for 3 to $3\frac{1}{2}$ hours or until internal temperature registers 200°F (100°C) on instant-read thermometer. Do not overbake. Let cool in pans on racks for 10 minutes. Remove cakes from pans and let cool completely on racks.

8. Carefully remove parchment when cakes have cooled completely. Wrap cakes airtight and store in the refrigerator for up to 2 months or in the freezer for up to 1 year.

Variation
Top cooled cakes with a thick layer of GF marzipan.

Blueberry Hazelnut Crumble Coffee Cake

Makes
9 to 12 servings

Blueberries add moisture and flavor to this cake, while hazelnuts give it a crunch. Here's an interesting food fact: in some areas, hazelnuts are known as filberts.

Tip
There is no need to thaw blueberries.

Variation
Substitute pecans for hazelnuts in topping. Substitute fresh or frozen cranberries for blueberries and omit hazelnuts in cake (see photo page 167).

- Stand mixer fitted with wire whisk attachment
- 9-inch (23 cm) square metal baking pan, lightly greased and bottom lined with parchment paper

Hazelnut Topping

¾ cup	finely chopped hazelnuts	175 mL
⅓ cup	packed brown sugar	75 mL
2 tbsp	amaranth flour	30 mL
3 tbsp	melted butter	45 mL

Coffee Cake

1¼ cups	sorghum flour	300 mL
½ cup	amaranth flour	125 mL
¼ cup	tapioca starch	60 mL
1½ tsp	xanthan gum	7 mL
1 tbsp	GF baking powder	15 mL
¼ tsp	salt	1 mL
1 tsp	ground nutmeg	5 mL
1	egg	1
½ cup	packed brown sugar	125 mL
2 tsp	grated lemon zest	10 mL
1 cup	milk	250 mL
¼ cup	vegetable oil	60 mL
2 cups	fresh or frozen blueberries	500 mL
1 cup	chopped hazelnuts	250 mL

1. *Hazelnut Topping:* In a small bowl, combine hazelnuts, brown sugar, amaranth flour and butter. Set aside.

2. *Coffee Cake:* In a large bowl or plastic bag, combine sorghum flour, amaranth flour, tapioca starch, xanthan gum, baking powder, salt and nutmeg. Mix well and set aside.

3. In mixer bowl, combine egg, brown sugar, lemon zest, milk and vegetable oil. With mixer on low speed, slowly add dry ingredients and mix until just combined. Gently fold in blueberries and hazelnuts.

4. Spoon batter into prepared pan. Using a moistened rubber spatula, spread to edges and smooth top. Sprinkle with topping. Let stand for 30 minutes.

5. Meanwhile, preheat oven to 350°F (180°C).

6. Bake for 30 to 40 minutes or until a tester inserted in the center comes out clean. Let cool in pan on a rack for 10 minutes. Remove from pan and let cool completely on rack.

Nutrients per serving

Calories	343
Fat	19 g
Saturated fat	3 g
Cholesterol	24 mg
Sodium	96 mg
Carbohydrate	40 g
Fiber	5 g
Protein	6 g
Calcium	125 mg
Iron	2 mg

Raspberry Jelly Roll

**Makes
10 to 12 servings**

This treat looks attractive and gourmet, but it is so easy to prepare. You will impress your GF friends and others.

Tips

See the Techniques Glossary, page 217, for information on folding in and warming egg whites.

Most new electric hand mixers have a wire whisk attachment, which will give you a better beating action, but a standard hand mixer works well, too.

For better volume when beating egg whites, make sure the mixer bowl and beaters are completely free of grease and egg yolk.

Nutrients per serving

Calories	173
Fat	4 g
Saturated fat	1 g
Cholesterol	61 mg
Sodium	48 mg
Carbohydrate	33 g
Fiber	1 g
Protein	3 g
Calcium	54 mg
Iron	0 mg

- Electric hand mixer fitted with wire whisk attachment (see Tips, at left)
- 15- by 10-inch (38 by 25 cm) rimmed baking sheet, lined with parchment paper

½ cup	almond flour	125 mL
2 tbsp	arrowroot starch	30 mL
2 tsp	baking powder	10 mL
1½ tsp	xanthan gum	7 mL
4	egg whites, at room temperature	4
¼ tsp	cream of tartar	1 mL
¾ cup	granulated sugar, divided	175 mL
4	egg yolks	4
⅛ tsp	salt	0.5 mL
½ tsp	almond extract	2 mL
	GF confectioners' (icing) sugar	
1 cup	raspberry jam	250 mL

1. In a small bowl, combine almond flour, arrowroot starch, baking powder and xanthan gum. Mix well and set aside.

2. In a large bowl, using electric hand mixer, beat egg whites until foamy. Beat in cream of tartar. Continue beating until egg whites are stiff. Gradually beat in ¼ cup (60 mL) granulated sugar. Continue beating until mixture is very stiff and glossy, but not dry. Set aside.

3. Meanwhile, preheat oven to 350°F (180°C).

4. In a small bowl, using electric hand mixer, beat egg yolks, the remaining ½ cup (125 mL) granulated sugar, salt and almond extract for about 5 minutes or until thick and lemon-colored.

5. Using a rubber spatula, fold egg yolk mixture into egg white mixture. Sprinkle with half dry ingredients and fold in gently. Repeat with the remaining half. Spoon mixture into prepared pan and carefully spread to edges.

Tip

Wrapped airtight, the jelly roll can be frozen for up to 1 month. Thaw, wrapped, in the refrigerator for several hours or overnight.

6. Bake in preheated oven for 10 to 12 minutes or until top springs back when lightly touched. Let cool on baking sheet on a rack for 5 minutes. Dust lightly with confectioners' sugar. Loosen edges of cake with a knife. Turn out onto a clean, lint-free tea towel set on rack and carefully remove parchment paper. Starting at a long side, roll up cake in the towel. Let cool on rack for 20 minutes.

7. Gently unroll cake, being careful not to flatten it. Spread with raspberry jam. Roll up again and place seam side down on a serving platter. Cover and refrigerate for 30 to 60 minutes, until chilled, or for up to 1 day.

Variation

Fill with chocolate or lemon curd for a less traditional dessert.

German Chocolate Cake

**Makes
9 to 12 servings**

Chocolate with
buttermilk smooths out
the flavor of this mild
chocolate cake.

Tip
Watch chocolate carefully
as it melts; don't let it get
completely melted in the
microwave.

Variation
Use sour milk instead
of buttermilk: combine
1 cup (250 mL) milk
and 1 tsp (5 mL) lemon
juice and let stand for
5 minutes.

- Electric hand mixer
- 9-inch (23 cm) square metal baking pan, lightly
  greased and bottom lined with parchment paper

⅔ cup	sorghum flour	150 mL
½ cup	teff flour	125 mL
3 tbsp	tapioca starch	45 mL
2 tsp	xanthan gum	10 mL
1 tbsp	GF baking powder	15 mL
½ tsp	baking soda	2 mL
½ tsp	salt	2 mL
3 oz	milk chocolate, chopped into small pieces	90 g
¼ cup	water	60 mL
¼ cup	butter, softened	60 mL
1	egg	1
⅔ cup	granulated sugar	150 mL
1 cup	buttermilk	250 mL
1 tsp	vanilla extract	5 mL

1. In a large bowl or plastic bag, combine sorghum flour, teff flour, tapioca starch, xanthan gum, baking powder, baking soda and salt. Mix well and set aside.

2. In a microwave-safe bowl, microwave chocolate and water, uncovered, on Medium for 60 to 90 seconds or until partially melted. Stir until completely melted. Let cool to room temperature.

3. In a separate bowl, using electric hand mixer, beat butter, egg, sugar, buttermilk and vanilla until combined. With mixer on low speed, mix in cooled melted chocolate until combined. Add dry ingredients and mix until just combined.

4. Spoon batter into prepared pan. Using a moistened rubber spatula, spread batter to edges and smooth top. Let stand for 30 minutes.

5. Meanwhile, preheat oven to 350°F (180°C).

6. Bake for 30 to 35 minutes or until a tester inserted in the center comes out clean. Let cool in pan on a rack for 10 minutes. Remove from pan and let cool completely on rack.

Nutrients per serving

Calories	187
Fat	7 g
Saturated fat	4 g
Cholesterol	29 mg
Sodium	215 mg
Carbohydrate	28 g
Fiber	2 g
Protein	4 g
Calcium	109 mg
Iron	1 mg

Red Velvet Cake

Makes 9 servings

While this is not a cake we grew up with ourselves, friends from the South insist it is a classic.

Tips

The amount of food coloring specified here will create a rich red cake. If you want a truly bright and blazing red cake, add more food coloring until the batter turns the desired shade of red.

Don't skip the sifting of the cocoa as it will lump.

- Electric hand mixer
- 8-inch (20 cm) square metal baking pan, lightly greased and bottom lined with parchment paper

¾ cup	sorghum flour	175 mL
½ cup	whole bean flour	125 mL
3 tbsp	cornstarch	45 mL
1 cup	granulated sugar	250 mL
1½ tsp	xanthan gum	7 mL
2 tsp	baking soda	10 mL
½ tsp	salt	2 mL
2 tbsp	unsweetened cocoa powder, sifted	30 mL
2	eggs	2
1¼ cups	buttermilk	300 mL
⅓ cup	vegetable oil	75 mL
2 tbsp	GF red food coloring	30 mL
2 tsp	cider vinegar	10 mL
1	recipe Red Velvet Frosting (page 173)	1

1. In a large bowl or plastic bag, combine sorghum flour, whole bean flour, cornstarch, sugar, xanthan gum, baking soda, salt and cocoa. Mix well and set aside.

2. In a separate bowl, using electric hand mixer, beat eggs, buttermilk, vegetable oil, food coloring and vinegar until combined. Add dry ingredients and mix until just combined.

3. Spoon batter evenly into prepared pan. Let stand for 30 minutes.

4. Meanwhile, preheat oven to 350°F (180°C).

5. Bake for 35 to 45 minutes or until a tester inserted in the center comes out clean.

6. Remove cake from oven. Let cool in pan on a rack for 10 minutes. Remove from pan and let cool completely on rack. Spread frosting on the top and sides of cake.

Nutrients per serving

Calories	275
Fat	11 g
Saturated fat	1 g
Cholesterol	44 mg
Sodium	456 mg
Carbohydrate	40 g
Fiber	3 g
Protein	6 g
Calcium	64 mg
Iron	2 mg

Cream Cheese Frosting

**Makes about
2 cups (500 mL)**

**(2 tbsp/30 mL
per serving)**

The only acceptable
finish for Carrot Cake
(page 160) is cream
cheese frosting.

Tip

Ices one cake in a 10-inch
(25 cm) bundt cake pan or a
13- by 9-inch (33 by 23 cm)
baking pan.

- **Electric hand mixer**

1	package (8 oz/250 g) brick cream cheese, at room temperature	1
¼ cup	butter, softened	60 mL
2 cups	sifted GF confectioners' (icing) sugar	500 mL
1 tsp	almond extract	5 mL

1. In a medium bowl, using electric hand mixer, beat cream cheese and butter until light and fluffy. Beat in confectioners' sugar and almond extract until blended.

2. Spread cream cheese frosting on the top and sides of cake.

Nutrients per serving

Calories	101	Carbohydrate	13 g
Fat	6 g	Fiber	0 g
Saturated fat	3 g	Protein	1 g
Cholesterol	19 mg	Calcium	8 mg
Sodium	68 mg	Iron	0 mg

Red Velvet Frosting

**Makes 1½ cups
(375 mL)**

**(2 tbsp/30 mL
per serving)**

Here is our version of
the traditional frosting
for Red Velvet Cake
(page 172).

Tips

Ices one 8-inch (20 cm) cake
or 12 cupcakes.

This frosting will have the
consistency of whipped cream.

- **Electric hand mixer**

2 tbsp	almond flour	30 mL
¼ to ½ cup	milk	60 mL to 125 mL
½ cup	granulated sugar	125 mL
½ cup	butter, softened	125 mL
½ tsp	almond extract	2 mL

1. In a small microwave-safe bowl, combine almond flour and milk. Microwave on High for 2 minutes, stopping to stir occasionally, until boiling and thickened. Let cool completely.

2. In a small bowl, using electric hand mixer, cream sugar, butter and almond extract until light and fluffy. Beat in almond flour milk mixture until light and fluffy.

Nutrients per serving

Calories	89	Carbohydrate	7 g
Fat	7 g	Fiber	0 g
Saturated fat	4 g	Protein	1 g
Cholesterol	17 mg	Calcium	14 mg
Sodium	58 mg	Iron	0 mg

Sponge Cake

Makes
12 to 16 servings

This light-textured cake is perfect topped with seasonal fresh fruit. It also can be used as a base for strawberry shortcake, instead of biscuits.

Tips

For better volume when beating egg whites, make sure the mixer bowl and beaters are completely free of grease and egg yolk.

Most new electric hand mixers have a wire whisk attachment, which will give you a better beating action, but a standard hand mixer works well, too.

For the best volume when whipping egg whites, be sure they are warmed to room temperature. See the Techniques Glossary, page 217.

To slice cake without squishing it, use dental floss or a knife with a serrated edge, such as an electric knife.

Nutrients per serving

Calories	104
Fat	3 g
Saturated fat	1 g
Cholesterol	58 mg
Sodium	82 mg
Carbohydrate	16 g
Fiber	1 g
Protein	4 g
Calcium	18 mg
Iron	1 mg

- Preheat oven to 350°F (180°C)
- Electric hand mixer fitted with wire whisk attachment (see Tips, at left)
- 13- by 9-inch (33 by 23 cm) metal baking pan, bottom lined with parchment paper

½ cup	amaranth flour	125 mL
¼ cup	almond flour	60 mL
½ cup	tapioca starch	125 mL
1½ tsp	xanthan gum	7 mL
12	egg whites, at room temperature	12
1 tbsp	freshly squeezed lemon juice	15 mL
1 tsp	almond extract	5 mL
½ tsp	cream of tartar	2 mL
¼ tsp	salt	1 mL
¾ cup	granulated sugar, divided	175 mL
5	egg yolks, at room temperature	5

1. In a small bowl or plastic bag, combine amaranth flour, almond flour, tapioca starch and xanthan gum. Mix well and set aside.

2. In a large bowl, using electric hand mixer, beat egg whites until foamy. Beat in lemon juice, almond extract, cream of tartar and salt. Continue beating until egg whites form stiff peaks. Gradually beat in ½ cup (125 mL) sugar. Continue beating until mixture is very stiff and glossy but not dry.

3. In a deep bowl, using electric hand mixer, beat egg yolks and the remaining ¼ cup (60 mL) sugar for about 5 minutes or until thick and lemon-colored.

4. Using a rubber spatula, fold egg yolk mixture into egg white mixture. Sift in dry ingredients, one-third at a time, gently folding in each addition until well blended. Spoon into prepared pan and carefully spread to edges.

5. Bake in preheated oven for 30 to 35 minutes or until cake is golden and springs back when lightly touched. Invert cake onto a rack, leaving pan on top, and let cool completely.

White Cake

Makes 9 servings

What a delicious cake, although the name is deceiving: it's creamier in color with a slight almond flavor.

Tips

When you're stirring in the dry ingredients alternately with the milk mixture, you can either use the electric hand mixer on low speed or switch to using a rubber spatula. Mix just until blended after each addition. This technique results in a more even-textured cake.

See the Techniques Glossary (page 218) for more information about tenting with foil.

Any leftover cake can be made into crumbs, frozen and used for crumb crusts.

Nutrients per serving

Calories	229
Fat	11 g
Saturated fat	5 g
Cholesterol	81 mg
Sodium	366 mg
Carbohydrate	29 g
Fiber	2 g
Protein	5 g
Calcium	105 mg
Iron	1 mg

- Electric hand mixer
- 8-inch (20 cm) square metal baking pan, lightly greased and bottom lined with parchment paper

⅔ cup	milk	150 mL
1 tsp	cider vinegar	5 mL
1 tsp	almond extract	5 mL
¾ cup	amaranth flour	175 mL
⅓ cup	almond flour	75 mL
3 tbsp	tapioca starch	45 mL
2 tsp	GF baking powder	10 mL
1 tsp	baking soda	5 mL
1½ tsp	xanthan gum	7 mL
½ tsp	salt	2 mL
⅓ cup	butter, softened	75 mL
¾ cup	granulated sugar	175 mL
3	large eggs	3

1. In a small bowl, combine milk, vinegar and almond extract; mix well. Let stand for 5 minutes.

2. In a bowl or plastic bag, combine amaranth flour, almond flour, tapioca starch, baking powder, baking soda, xanthan gum and salt. Mix well and set aside.

3. In a separate bowl, using electric hand mixer, cream butter until fluffy. Gradually beat in sugar. Continue beating until light and fluffy. Add eggs, one at a time, beating well after each. Stir in dry ingredients alternately with milk mixture, making three additions of dry and two of milk mixture.

4. Spoon batter into prepared pan. Using a moistened rubber spatula, spread to edges and smooth top. Let stand for 30 minutes.

5. Meanwhile, preheat oven to 350°F (180°C).

6. Bake for 18 minutes. Check to see if cake is getting too dark and tent with foil if necessary. Bake for 8 to 12 minutes or until a tester inserted in the center comes out clean. Let cool in pan on a rack for 5 minutes. Remove from pan and let cool completely on rack.

Variation

For a lighter-textured cake, separate eggs and beat whites until stiff but not dry, then fold into batter as the last step before spooning batter into baking pan.

Lemon Meringue Pie

Pies and
Pastry

Classic Pastry Two Ways 180

Pecan Pastry Two Ways 182

Apple Crumble Pie. 184

Butter Tarts. 186

Lemon Meringue Pie 188

Pumpkin Pie 189

Pecan Pie. 190

Pastry Tips

- There are two styles of pie dough: flaky and mealy. Decide which you prefer before you start mixing — you can create either using the same ingredients, but with different mixing techniques.

- **Flaky pie dough** must be mixed by hand, and the fat must be rubbed or cut into the dry ingredients with two knives or a pastry blender until the fat particles are pea-sized. The cold liquid mixture is then added slowly and absorbed by the dry ingredients. When rolled out, the small pieces of flour and fat create the "flakes" of this pastry. We like this pastry for dessert pies.

- **Mealy pie dough** is mixed more completely to the crumb stage. A food processor does this well. This type of dough is ideal for pies that tend to have a soggy bottom or to prepare as a crust for an entrée pie because the dry ingredients are coated completely with fat, so the crust is unable to absorb moisture. Sometimes, you might need slightly less water than the recipe calls for, so add it slowly and do not let the mixture overprocess.

Rules to Follow When Choosing Your Fat

- Room temperature shortening is very easy to rub or cut into the dry ingredients, resulting in a very flaky crust; however, it lacks flavor. Cold butter results in a more flavorful crust, but is often tough because it is more difficult to work into the dry ingredients and contains slightly more water. We prefer a 50/50 mix of butter to shortening, so we get the best of both fats.

- Butter contains more water than shortening, so decrease the liquid slightly if using butter in place of shortening.

- Substituting all butter into a recipe that calls for all shortening means the amount of butter must be increased by about 25%. Therefore, 1 cup (250 mL) shortening will become 1 ¼ cups (300 mL) butter.

Making Pastry

- In some recipes, we provide directions for using both the food processor and traditional methods of making pastry. When selecting the food processor method, pulse the ingredients until the dough begins to stick together. With your fingertips, gather the dough into a light ball and gently press it together.

- In the traditional method, use a pastry blender or two knives to cut in the fat until the pieces are the size of small peas. This results in a tender, flaky pastry. If the fat is too finely cut in or mashed, the pastry tends to be tough and heavy.

- Pastry is more tender when you use ice water, rather than tap water. To prepare the ice water, we add ice cubes to a small dish of water, then measure out the recipe amount once it is ice-cold.

- Form the dough into round, flattened discs before chilling. This shape is easier to roll out into a circle.

- Refrigerate the dough, tightly wrapped, for at least 1 hour before rolling it out. It can be stored in the refrigerator for up to 3 days or in the freezer for up to 3 months. Thaw frozen pastry overnight in the refrigerator before rolling out.

- Roll out the dough between two sheets of parchment paper — it is easier to handle that way.

- Roll out the dough using light, long strokes from the center to the edges. Roll out to each side, then back to the center. Repeat until the dough is the desired size or thickness.

- Ease the pastry into the pan. Do not worry if it breaks where it touches the rim; just patch the shell with pastry scraps.

Classic Pastry Two Ways

Makes one 9-inch (23 cm) shell

Choose either of these methods, depending on what you are baking. The food processor method works best for our Chicken Pot Pie (page 76).

Tips

To ensure success, see page 179 for tips on making pastry.

Double the recipe for a two-crust pie.

Pastry can be stored in the refrigerator for up to 3 days or in the freezer for up to 3 months. Thaw frozen pastry overnight in the refrigerator before rolling out.

Nutrients per serving

Calories	350
Fat	22 g
Saturated fat	10 g
Cholesterol	77 mg
Sodium	253 mg
Carbohydrate	37 g
Fiber	2 g
Protein	2 g
Calcium	12 mg
Iron	1 mg

Food Processor Method

- **Food processor**

2	egg yolks	2
⅓ cup	ice water	75 mL
1 tsp	cider vinegar	5 mL
1 cup	brown rice flour	250 mL
1 cup	cornstarch	250 mL
½ cup	tapioca starch	125 mL
2 tsp	xanthan gum	10 mL
½ tsp	salt	2 mL
½ cup	butter	125 mL
⅓ cup	shortening	75 mL

1. In a small bowl, whisk together egg yolks, ice water and vinegar. Refrigerate until needed.

2. In food processor fitted with metal blade, pulse rice flour, cornstarch, tapioca starch, xanthan gum and salt until combined.

3. Add butter and shortening, and pulse for 5 to 10 seconds or until mixture resembles small peas. With motor running, add egg yolk mixture in a slow, steady stream; pulse until dough just holds together. Do not let it form a ball.

4. Gently gather into a ball and flatten into a disc about 6 inches (15 cm) in diameter. Wrap disc in plastic wrap and place in a plastic bag. Refrigerate for at least 1 hour, until chilled, or overnight.

5. Unwrap disc and place it on a sheet of parchment paper. Cover with another sheet of parchment paper. Roll out dough into a circle about 1 inch (2.5 cm) larger than the diameter of an inverted pie pan. Carefully remove top sheet of parchment paper and invert pastry over pie pan, easing it in. Carefully peel off remaining sheet of parchment paper.

6. Trim excess pastry to edge of pan and patch any cracks with trimmings. Using a sharp knife, trim edges evenly.

7. *To Bake Unfilled Pastry Shell:* To prevent pastry from shrinking or puffing up, prick bottom and sides with a fork. Bake at 425°F (220°C) for 18 to 20 minutes or until golden. Let cool completely before filling.

8. *To Bake Filled Pastry Shell:* Do not prick pastry. Spoon filling into unbaked pastry shells and bake according to individual recipe instructions.

Traditional Method

2	egg yolks	2
1/3 cup	ice water	75 mL
1 tsp	cider vinegar	5 mL
1 cup	brown rice flour	250 mL
1 cup	cornstarch	250 mL
1/2 cup	tapioca starch	125 mL
2 tsp	xanthan gum	10 mL
1/2 tsp	salt	2 mL
1/2 cup	butter	125 mL
1/3 cup	shortening	75 mL

1. In a small bowl, whisk together egg yolks, ice water and vinegar. Refrigerate until needed.

2. In a large bowl, combine rice flour, cornstarch, tapioca starch, xanthan gum and salt. Using a pastry blender or two knives, cut in butter and shortening until mixture resembles small peas. Sprinkle egg yolk mixture, a little at a time, over flour mixture, stirring with a fork until a soft dough forms.

3. Gently gather into a ball and flatten into a disc 6 inches (15 cm) in diameter. Wrap disc in plastic wrap and place in a plastic bag. Refrigerate for at least 1 hour, until chilled, or overnight.

4. Unwrap disc and place it on a sheet of parchment paper. Cover with another sheet of parchment paper. Roll out dough into a circle about 1 inch (2.5 cm) larger than the diameter of an inverted pie pan. Carefully remove top sheet of parchment paper and invert pastry over pie pan, easing it in. Carefully peel off remaining sheet of parchment paper.

5. Trim excess pastry to edge of pan and patch any cracks with trimmings. Using a sharp knife, trim edges evenly.

6. *To Bake Unfilled Pastry Shell:* To prevent pastry from shrinking or puffing up, prick bottom and sides with a fork. Bake at 425°F (220°C) for 18 to 20 minutes or until golden. Let cool completely before filling.

7. *To Bake Filled Pastry Shell:* Do not prick pastry. Spoon filling into unbaked pastry shells and bake according to individual recipe instructions.

Pecan Pastry Two Ways

Makes one 9-inch (23 cm) pie shell or 12 tarts

This is one of our favorites for the crust of a Pecan Pie (page 190) or Butter Tarts (page 186).

Tips

To ensure success, see page 179 for tips on making pastry.

Work quickly to keep pastry cold and prevent butter from softening.

Pastry can be stored in the refrigerator for up to 3 days or in the freezer for up to 3 months. Thaw frozen pastry overnight in the refrigerator before rolling out.

Food Processor Method

• **Food processor**

2	egg yolks	2
1/3 cup	ice water	75 mL
1 tsp	cider vinegar	5 mL
1 cup	sorghum flour	250 mL
1/2 cup	pecan flour	125 mL
2/3 cup	cornstarch	150 mL
1/3 cup	tapioca starch	75 mL
2 tsp	xanthan gum	10 mL
1/4 tsp	salt	1 mL
3/4 cup	cold butter, cut into 1/2-inch (1 cm) cubes	175 mL

1. In a small bowl, whisk together egg yolks, ice water and vinegar. Set aside.

2. In food processor fitted with metal blade, pulse sorghum flour, pecan flour, cornstarch, tapioca starch, xanthan gum and salt until combined. Add butter and pulse for 10 to 20 seconds or until mixture resembles small peas. With motor running, add egg yolk mixture in a slow, steady stream; pulse until dough just holds together. Do not let it form a ball.

3. Gently gather dough into a ball and flatten into a disc 6 inches (15 cm) in diameter. Wrap disc in plastic wrap and place in a plastic bag. Refrigerate for at least 1 hour, until chilled, or overnight.

4. Remove disc from the refrigerator. Unwrap disc and place it on a sheet of parchment paper. Cover with another sheet of parchment paper. Let stand for 5 to 10 minutes. Roll out dough into a circle about 1 inch (2.5 cm) larger than the diameter of a pie pan. Carefully remove top sheet of parchment paper and invert pastry over pan, easing it in. Carefully peel off remaining sheet of parchment paper.

5. Trim excess pastry to edge of pan and patch any cracks with trimmings. Moisten fingers in cold water to prevent sticking while patching cracks. Using a sharp knife, trim edges evenly.

6. *To Bake Unfilled Pastry Shell:* To prevent pastry from shrinking or puffing up, prick bottom and sides with a fork. Bake at 425°F (220°C) for 18 to 20 minutes or until golden. Let cool completely before filling.

7. *To Bake Filled Pastry Shell:* Do not prick pastry. Spoon filling into unbaked pastry shell and bake according to individual recipe directions.

Nutrients per serving

Calories	310
Fat	22 g
Saturated fat	12 g
Cholesterol	92 mg
Sodium	79 mg
Carbohydrate	28 g
Fiber	3 g
Protein	3 g
Calcium	16 mg
Iron	1 mg

Variations

If pecan flour is not readily available, make your own (see the Techniques Glossary, page 217). Or substitute hazelnut flour or almond flour.

Galette: Preheat oven to 425°F (220°C). Follow directions to prepare dough by either method, then form dough into a free-form circle and top with a fresh fruit filling within 2 inches (5 cm) of edge. Carefully fold pastry up over filling to form a ragged edge, leaving fruit exposed in center. Sprinkle pastry with 1 tbsp (15 mL) sugar. Bake in preheated oven for 15 minutes. Reduce heat to 375°F (190°C) and bake for 25 to 30 minutes longer or until fruit is tender and pastry is lightly browned.

Traditional Method

2	egg yolks	2
1/3 cup	ice water	75 mL
1 tsp	cider vinegar	5 mL
1 cup	sorghum flour	250 mL
1/2 cup	pecan flour	125 mL
2/3 cup	cornstarch	150 mL
1/3 cup	tapioca starch	75 mL
2 tsp	xanthan gum	10 mL
1/4 tsp	salt	1 mL
3/4 cup	cold butter, cut into 1/2-inch (1 cm) cubes	175 mL

1. In a small bowl, whisk together egg yolks, ice water and vinegar. Set aside.

2. In a large bowl, combine sorghum flour, pecan flour, cornstarch, tapioca starch, xanthan gum and salt.

3. Using a pastry blender or two knives, cut in butter until mixture resembles small peas. Sprinkle egg yolk mixture, a little at a time, over flour mixture, stirring with a fork until a soft dough forms.

4. Gently gather dough into a ball and flatten into a disc 6 inches (15 cm) in diameter. Wrap disc in plastic wrap and place in a plastic bag. Refrigerate for at least 1 hour, until chilled, or overnight.

5. Remove disc from the refrigerator. Unwrap disc and place it on a sheet of parchment paper. Cover with another sheet of parchment paper. Let stand for 5 to 10 minutes. Roll out dough into a circle about 1 inch (2.5 cm) larger than the diameter of a pie pan. Carefully remove top sheet of parchment paper and invert pastry over pan, easing it in. Carefully peel off remaining sheet of parchment paper.

6. Trim excess pastry to edge of pan and patch any cracks with trimmings. Moisten fingers in cold water to prevent sticking while patching cracks. Using a sharp knife, trim edges evenly.

7. *To Bake Unfilled Pastry Shell*: To prevent pastry from shrinking or puffing up, prick bottom and sides with a fork. Bake at 425°F (220°C) for 18 to 20 minutes or until golden. Let cool completely before filling.

8. *To Bake Filled Pastry Shell*: Do not prick pastry. Spoon filling into unbaked pastry shell and bake according to individual recipe directions.

Apple Crumble Pie

Makes 8 servings

This classic pie, served warm with sharp (old) Cheddar cheese, will bring calls for seconds from everyone.

Tips

Seven medium apples yield approximately 6 cups (1.5 L) sliced. Select a blend of apples, rather than just one variety. Some apples remain firm, while others become mushy. Some diminish in flavor from baking, while others actually improve. For baking, we suggest equal parts of both tart apples, such as Granny Smith or Cortland, and sweet apples, including Yellow Delicious or Braeburn.

- **Preheat oven to 400°F (200°C)**

Crumble Topping

½ cup	amaranth flour	125 mL
¼ cup	tapioca starch	60 mL
½ cup	packed brown sugar	125 mL
1 tbsp	ground cinnamon	15 mL
½ cup	butter, melted	125 mL

Filling

6 cups	peeled, cored and sliced apples (see Tips, at left)	1.5 L
¼ cup	packed brown sugar	60 mL
¼ cup	granulated sugar	60 mL
2 tbsp	amaranth flour	30 mL
½ tsp	ground cinnamon	2 mL
1	recipe Classic Pastry (page 180), unbaked	1

1. *Crumble Topping:* In a small bowl, combine amaranth flour, tapioca starch, brown sugar, cinnamon and butter. Stir with a fork until crumbly. Set aside.

2. *Filling:* In a large bowl, combine apples, brown sugar, sugar, amaranth flour and cinnamon. Mix gently. Spoon into pastry shell. Top with crumble mixture. Do not pack.

3. Bake in preheated oven for 10 minutes. Reduce oven temperature to 350°F (180°C) and bake for an additional 20 to 25 minutes or until topping is lightly browned, filling is bubbly and apples are fork-tender. Let cool completely on rack.

Variation

In Step 2, top with a second unbaked Classic Pastry shell, rather than with crumble topping. Seal around edge, then cut steam slits in top and bake at 425°F (220°C) for 15 minutes. Reduce oven temperature to 350°F (180°C) and bake for 35 to 40 minutes or until apples are tender and crust is golden. Let cool completely on rack.

Nutrients per serving

Calories	653
Fat	34 g
Saturated fat	17 g
Cholesterol	107 mg
Sodium	364 mg
Carbohydrate	87 g
Fiber	6 g
Protein	4 g
Calcium	62 mg
Iron	2 mg

Butter Tarts

Makes 12 tarts
(1 per serving)

Everyone knows that Canada makes the best butter tarts, and I don't know anyone who doesn't love them.

Tip

To prevent butter tarts from bubbling over as they bake, stir filling as little as possible before spooning it into shells.

- 12-cup tart or muffin pan
- Preheat oven to 350°F (180°C)

1	recipe Pecan Pastry (page 182), unbaked	1
1 cup	packed brown sugar	250 mL
¾ cup	corn syrup	175 mL
½ cup	butter, melted and cooled slightly	125 mL
¼ cup	vegetable oil	60 mL
½ tsp	vanilla extract	2 mL
3	eggs, lightly beaten	3

1. Using a sharp knife, cut pastry in half; cut each half in half and then each quarter into thirds. You will have 12 equal portions. Wrap each in plastic. Refrigerate for 1 hour or overnight.

2. Remove one portion at a time, keeping the remaining portions cold until needed. Place on parchment paper and cover with a second sheet of parchment paper. Roll out dough into a circle about 1 inch (2.5 cm) larger than the diameter of the cup of inverted tart pan. Carefully remove top sheet of parchment paper and ease dough into cup. Carefully peel off remaining sheet of parchment paper. Repeat with the remaining portions. Using a sharp knife, trim edges evenly and patch any cracks with trimmings.

3. In a bowl, combine brown sugar, corn syrup, butter, vegetable oil and vanilla. Add eggs and mix just until blended.

4. Spoon mixture into tart shells, filling only two-thirds full. Bake in preheated oven for 15 to 18 minutes or until filling is puffed and set. Let cool completely on a rack before removing from pan.

Variations

Stir 1 cup (250 mL) raisins or chopped pecans into mixture before filling tart shells.

Choose either Classic Pastry (page 180) or Pecan Pastry (page 182) if adding pecans to tarts.

Chocolatey Butter Tarts: Top each tart with 2 tsp (10 mL) coarsely chopped bittersweet (dark) chocolate just before baking.

Nutrients per serving

Calories	466
Fat	28 g
Saturated fat	13 g
Cholesterol	128 mg
Sodium	157 mg
Carbohydrate	54 g
Fiber	2 g
Protein	4 g
Calcium	38 mg
Iron	1 mg

Lemon Meringue Pie

Makes 8 servings

This is the perfect recipe for those who love a classic made from scratch.

Tips

Most new electric hand mixers have a wire whisk attachment, which will give you a better beating action, but a standard hand mixer works well, too.

It is worth the time and effort to squeeze a fresh lemon, rather than use bottled juice.

Seal meringue to pastry's edge or it will shrink, and the heat from the oven will cause the filling to become thin and watery.

Nutrients per serving

Calories	530
Fat	28 g
Saturated fat	13 g
Cholesterol	157 mg
Sodium	298 mg
Carbohydrate	68 g
Fiber	2 g
Protein	3 g
Calcium	25 mg
Iron	1 mg

- Preheat oven to 400°F (200°C)
- Electric hand mixer fitted with wire whisk attachment (see Tips, at left)

Filling

1 cup	granulated sugar	250 mL
1/3 cup	cornstarch	75 mL
2 cups	water	500 mL
1 tsp	grated lemon zest	5 mL
1/2 cup	freshly squeezed lemon juice	125 mL
3 tbsp	butter	45 mL
3	egg yolks, lightly beaten	3
1	recipe Classic Pastry (page 180), baked	1

Meringue

3	egg whites, at room temperature	3
1/4 tsp	cream of tartar	1 mL
1/4 cup	granulated sugar	60 mL

1. *Filling:* In a saucepan, combine sugar and cornstarch. Stir in water, lemon zest, lemon juice and butter.

2. Cook over medium heat, stirring constantly, for 5 to 8 minutes or until mixture boils and thickens.

3. In a small bowl, beat egg yolks. Gradually whisk in half of sugar mixture until well blended. Pour egg mixture into saucepan and stir until combined. Remove from heat and let cool for 5 minutes, then pour into pie shell.

4. *Meringue:* In a separate bowl, using electric hand mixer, beat egg whites and cream of tartar on high until soft peaks form. Very gradually beat in sugar.

5. Top pie with meringue. Using the back of a spoon, seal meringue to edges of pastry. Bake in preheated oven for 5 to 6 minutes or until meringue is golden. Let cool completely on a rack. Serve immediately or refrigerate for up to 1 day.

Variation

You could also use baked Pecan Pastry (page 182) for this recipe.

Pumpkin Pie

Makes 8 servings

How can you enjoy Thanksgiving dinner without a slice of pumpkin pie?

Tips

One 14 oz/398 mL can contains 1½ cups (375 mL) pumpkin purée. Substitute your own homemade purée if desired.

Baking the crust slightly before adding filling ensures the crust is baked and not soggy.

1	recipe Classic Pastry (page 180), unbaked	1
3	eggs	3
1	can (14 oz/398 mL) 100% pure pumpkin	1
¾ cup	packed brown sugar	175 mL
¾ cup	half-and-half (10%) cream	175 mL
1 tsp	ground cinnamon	5 mL
½ tsp	cloves	2 mL
½ tsp	ground ginger	2 mL
½ tsp	ground nutmeg	2 mL
¼ tsp	salt	1 mL

1. In a large bowl, combine eggs, pumpkin, brown sugar, cream, cinnamon, cloves, ginger, nutmeg and salt. Set aside.

2. Bake pastry shell for 10 minutes. Cool until set. Add filling and bake for 15 minutes. Reduce oven temperature to 350°F (180°C) and bake for 40 to 50 minutes or until set. The tip of a knife inserted into the center should come out clean. Let cool completely on a rack.

Variations

Use evaporated milk for half-and-half (10%) cream.

Add ½ tsp (2 mL) ground allspice instead of ginger.

Some 9-inch (23 cm) pie pans hold more than others. If your pie pan is shallow, you might have extra filling. Bake extra in a small greased casserole dish at the same time as the pie, checking occasionally for doneness. It will take between 15 and 39 minutes, depending on the size and depth of the dish.

Nutrients per serving

Calories	503
Fat	26 g
Saturated fat	12 g
Cholesterol	155 mg
Sodium	371 mg
Carbohydrate	63 g
Fiber	3 g
Protein	6 g
Calcium	81 mg
Iron	2 mg

Pecan Pie

Makes 8 servings

It doesn't matter whether you grew up in the North or the South — everyone loves pecan pie.

Tip

To prevent pecan pie from bubbling over and remaining liquid in the center, stir filling as little as possible.

• **Preheat oven to 375°F (190°C)**

⅔ cup	packed brown sugar	150 mL
½ cup	corn syrup	125 mL
⅓ cup	butter, melted and cooled slightly	75 mL
½ tsp	vanilla extract	2 mL
3	eggs, lightly beaten	3
1	recipe Pecan Pastry (page 182), unbaked	1
1¼ cups	whole pecans or pecan pieces	300 mL

1. In a medium bowl, combine brown sugar, corn syrup, butter and vanilla. Add eggs and mix until just blended.

2. Pour filling into unbaked pastry shell, filling two-thirds full. Top with whole pecans formed into ever-smaller circles or sprinkle with pecan pieces.

3. Bake in preheated oven for 10 minutes. Reduce oven temperature to 325°F (160°C) and bake for an additional 20 to 25 minutes or until filling is golden brown and set. Let cool completely on a rack.

Variation

Substitute 2 tbsp (30 mL) dark rum for vanilla extract. This tends to cut the sweetness.

Nutrients per serving

Calories	644
Fat	42 g
Saturated fat	18 g
Cholesterol	182 mg
Sodium	192 mg
Carbohydrate	65 g
Fiber	4 g
Protein	7 g
Calcium	58 mg
Iron	2 mg

Christmas Pudding with Toffee Sauce

Puddings and Other Sweets

Apple Crisp. 194

Crêpes. 196

Crêpes Suzette. 198

Creamy Rice Pudding. 199

Chocolate Pudding Cake 200

Christmas Pudding 202

Toffee Sauce 203

New York–Style Cheesecake. 204

Doughnuts. 206

Lemon Snow with Raspberry Coulis 208

Apple Crisp

Makes 6 to 8 servings

An apple crisp is one of our favorite ways to use up a basket of fruit. Make several crisps when the fruit is plentiful, and freeze them to enjoy in late fall.

Tips

We like to leave the peel on, but remove it if you want.

To store, let cool completely, wrap airtight and freeze for up to 3 months.

1½ lbs (750 g) apples yield 6 cups (1.5 L) thickly sliced apples.

Two medium apples yield about 1½ cups (375 mL) thickly sliced apples.

- Preheat oven to 350°F (180°C)
- 8-cup (2 L) casserole dish, lightly greased

Base

6 cups	baking apples, cored and cut into thick slices	1.5 L
3 tbsp	sorghum flour	45 mL
2 tbsp	packed brown sugar	30 mL

Topping

1½ cups	GF large-flake (old-fashioned) rolled oats	375 mL
⅓ cup	sorghum flour	75 mL
¼ cup	packed brown sugar	60 mL
1 tsp	ground cinnamon	5 mL
⅓ cup	butter, melted	75 mL

1. *Base:* In prepared casserole dish, gently combine apples, sorghum flour and brown sugar. Set aside.

2. *Topping:* In a bowl, combine oats, sorghum flour, brown sugar and cinnamon. Drizzle with butter and mix with a fork just until crumbly. Sprinkle over apples. Do not pack.

3. Bake in preheated oven for 45 to 50 minutes or until bubbly around edges, topping is browned and apples are fork-tender. Serve warm.

Variation

Choose any variety of baking apple — Granny Smith, Northern Spy, Spartan, Golden Delicious or McIntosh are our favorites.

Nutrients per serving

Calories	302
Fat	10 g
Saturated fat	5 g
Cholesterol	20 mg
Sodium	72 mg
Carbohydrate	49 g
Fiber	6 g
Protein	6 g
Calcium	36 mg
Iron	2 mg

Crêpes

**Makes 12 crêpes
(2 per serving)**

Prepare these crêpes
ahead of time to make
entertaining a breeze.
Choose your favorite
filling, either sweet
or savory.

- 6-inch (15 cm) crêpe pan or nonstick skillet, lightly greased

⅓ cup	amaranth flour	75 mL
⅓ cup	teff flour	75 mL
3 tbsp	tapioca starch	45 mL
1 tbsp	granulated sugar	15 mL
½ tsp	xanthan gum	2 mL
½ tsp	salt	2 mL
3	eggs	3
1 cup	water	250 mL
⅓ cup	milk	75 mL
2 tbsp	melted butter, cooled slightly	30 mL

1. In a large bowl or plastic bag, mix together amaranth flour, teff flour, tapioca starch, sugar, xanthan gum and salt.

2. In a small bowl, whisk together eggs, water, milk and butter. Pour mixture over dry ingredients all at once, whisking until smooth. Cover and refrigerate for at least 1 hour or for up to 2 days.

3. Bring batter back to room temperature before making crêpes (takes about 1 hour).

4. Heat prepared pan over medium-high heat until a drop of water beads up and dances across the pan. Add 3 to 4 tbsp (45 to 60 mL) batter, tilting and rotating pan to ensure batter covers entire bottom. Cook for 1 minute or until edges just begin to brown. Turn carefully with a non-metal spatula. Cook for another 30 to 45 seconds. Transfer to a plate and repeat with the remaining batter.

Nutrients per serving

Calories	146
Fat	7 g
Saturated fat	3 g
Cholesterol	104 mg
Sodium	273 mg
Carbohydrate	16 g
Fiber	2 g
Protein	5 g
Calcium	53 mg
Iron	2 mg

Variations

Chocolate Crêpes:
In Step 1, increase granulated sugar to 3 tbsp (45 mL) and add ¼ cup (60 mL) sifted unsweetened cocoa powder.

Crêpes can be filled with chicken or seafood in a cream sauce for a savory lunch, or apple or blueberry for a sweet dessert.

Tips for Making and Storing Crêpes

The batter should be smooth and lump-free.

Refrigerate batter for at least 1 hour before making crêpes. This stabilizes the batter, making for more tender crêpes.

A well-seasoned crêpe pan should only need to be greased very lightly. Wipe out any excess with a paper towel. Too much grease on the pan results in greasy crêpes.

To test a nonstick crêpe pan or skillet for the correct temperature (375°F/190°C), sprinkle a few drops of water on the hot surface. If the water bounces and dances across the pan, it is ready to use. If the water sizzles and evaporates, it is too hot.

The secret to making perfect crêpes is simple: practice, practice, practice! In fact, the first crêpe of every batch is just that — a practice one that is meant to be thrown out.

If crêpes stick to the pan, let pan cool slightly, then regrease. Wipe out any excess with a paper towel. Reheat pan before making another crêpe.

As each crêpe is cooked, stack them between sheets of parchment or waxed paper.

Keep crêpes separated with parchment or waxed paper, wrap airtight and store in the refrigerator for up to 3 days or in the freezer for up to 1 month. To prevent tearing, thaw frozen crêpes in the refrigerator for at least 4 hours before separating them.

Crêpes Suzette

Makes 12 crêpes
(2 per serving)

Crêpes Suzette is a French dessert consisting of a crêpe with Beurre Suzette, a sauce of caramelized sugar and butter, orange juice, zest and orange liqueur on top, prepared in a tableside performance, flambé. Warm to room temperature and finish at the table.

Tips

For the orange liqueur, we like to use Grand Marnier, orange Curaçao or Cointreau.

If you want lots of sauce, double the recipe.

- 6-inch (15 cm) crêpe pan or nonstick skillet, lightly greased

1	recipe Crêpes (page 196)	1
1/3 cup	butter	75 mL
1/2 cup	frozen orange juice concentrate, thawed	125 mL
1/2 cup	orange liqueur	125 mL
1 tbsp	orange zest	15 mL
1 tbsp	liquid honey	15 mL
1/4 cup	brandy	60 mL

1. In crêpe pan or nonstick skillet, melt butter over medium heat. Add orange juice, orange liqueur, orange zest and honey.

2. Add one crêpe and spoon sauce over crêpe until well saturated. Using a small, heatproof spatula, gently fold crêpe in half and then into quarters. Gently remove to a heatproof dish. Repeat with remaining crêpes. Pour any remaining sauce over crêpes.

3. In a small saucepan, over medium-low heat, warm brandy just until heated through but not boiling. Remove from heat. Using a long match, ignite brandy; immediately pour over crêpes in dish.

Nutrients per serving

Calories	361
Fat	17 g
Saturated fat	10 g
Cholesterol	131 mg
Sodium	365 mg
Carbohydrate	35 g
Fiber	2 g
Protein	6 g
Calcium	64 mg
Iron	2 mg

Creamy Rice Pudding

**Makes 5 servings
(½ cup/125 mL
per serving)**

This used to be Donna's
favorite dessert
when she visited her
grandmother. The
stovetop method results
in a creamier pudding
than an oven-baked
pudding.

Tip
For an extra-creamy
pudding, choose short-grain
rice such as Arborio.

½ cup	short-grain rice	125 mL
3 cups	milk	750 mL
3 tbsp	granulated sugar	45 mL
1 tbsp	butter	15 mL
⅛ tsp	salt	0.5 mL
1 tsp	vanilla extract	5 mL
⅛ tsp	ground nutmeg	0.5 mL
½ cup	raisins	125 mL

1. In a large saucepan over medium heat, combine rice, milk, sugar, butter and salt. Cook, stirring often, until tiny bubbles form around edge, about 4 to 6 minutes. Reduce heat to low. Cover and simmer, stirring occasionally, for 1 hour or until rice is tender. Remove from heat. Stir in vanilla, nutmeg and raisins. Serve warm or chilled.

Variations
Substitute brown rice for short-grain white and increase cooking time by 45 minutes or until rice is tender. Increase milk to 4 cups (1 L).

Substitute ½ tsp (2 mL) ground cinnamon for nutmeg and chopped dates for raisins.

Nutrients per serving

Calories	188
Fat	3 g
Saturated fat	2 g
Cholesterol	9 mg
Sodium	44 mg
Carbohydrate	37 g
Fiber	1 g
Protein	3 g
Calcium	70 mg
Iron	1 mg

Chocolate Pudding Cake

Makes 4 servings

A comfort on the coldest winter day, this old-fashioned, self-saucing dessert was all the rage in the '50s. We've updated the recipe so that it uses less sugar and salt, but we've kept the flavor.

Tips

When boiling the water, heat extra and measure it after it has come to a boil. It may continue to bubble when removed from stovetop or microwave.

Variation

Spoon batter into 6-cup (1.5 L) lightly greased casserole dish. Complete Step 3. Bake for 40 to 50 minutes.

Nutrients per serving

Calories	336
Fat	2 g
Saturated fat	0 g
Cholesterol	4 mg
Sodium	121 mg
Carbohydrate	77 g
Fiber	4 g
Protein	6 g
Calcium	275 mg
Iron	4 mg

- Preheat oven to 350°F (180°C)
- Electric hand mixer
- Four 10-oz (300 mL) ovenproof ramekins, lightly greased
- Rimmed baking sheet

Cake

¼ cup	sorghum flour	60 mL
¼ cup	teff flour	60 mL
2 tbsp	tapioca starch	30 mL
½ cup	granulated sugar	125 mL
1 tbsp	GF baking powder	15 mL
1 tsp	xanthan gum	5 mL
⅛ tsp	salt	0.5 mL
¼ cup	sifted unsweetened cocoa powder	60 mL
1 cup	milk	250 mL
¼ tsp	vanilla extract	1 mL

Chocolate Sauce

½ cup	packed brown sugar	125 mL
2 tbsp	sifted unsweetened cocoa powder	30 mL
1 cup	boiling water	250 mL

1. *Cake:* In a medium bowl or plastic bag, combine sorghum flour, teff flour, tapioca starch, sugar, baking powder, xanthan gum, salt and cocoa. Mix well and set aside.

2. In a separate large bowl, using electric hand mixer, combine milk and vanilla. Gradually add dry ingredients and mix just until combined. Spoon into prepared ramekins, dividing mixture evenly. Place ramekins on rimmed baking sheet.

3. *Sauce:* In a small bowl, combine brown sugar and cocoa. Sprinkle evenly over batter. Holding a large spoon bowl-side down over center of batter, slowly pour boiling water evenly over ramekins. (The liquid will flow over the back of the spoon to distribute evenly.) Do not stir.

4. Bake in preheated oven for 30 to 35 minutes or until cake is firm when gently touched. Serve warm.

Christmas Pudding

**Makes
9 to 12 servings**

This is the dessert on
every Christmas menu at
both Heather and Donna's
homes. Serve warm
with lots of Toffee Sauce
(page 203).

Tips

When purchasing prechopped
dates, check for wheat starch
in the coating.

Instead of chopping dates
with a knife, simply snip
with scissors. When scissors
become sticky, just dip them
in hot water.

- Electric hand mixer
- 9-inch (23 cm) square metal baking pan, lightly greased

1½ cups	coarsely snipped pitted dates	375 mL
1 cup	water	250 mL
½ cup	sorghum flour	125 mL
½ cup	quinoa flour	125 mL
¼ cup	tapioca starch	60 mL
1½ tsp	GF baking powder	7 mL
1½ tsp	xanthan gum	7 mL
1 tsp	baking soda	5 mL
Pinch	salt	Pinch
⅓ cup	butter, softened	75 mL
¾ cup	packed brown sugar	175 mL
1 tsp	vanilla extract	5 mL
2	eggs	2

1. In a small saucepan, combine dates and water and bring to
   a boil over high heat. Reduce heat to medium and simmer
   until softened, about 5 minutes. Remove from heat and
   let cool to room temperature.

2. In a large bowl or plastic bag, mix together sorghum flour,
   quinoa flour, tapioca starch, baking powder, xanthan gum,
   baking soda and salt. Set aside.

3. In a large bowl, using electric hand mixer, cream butter.
   Gradually add brown sugar and beat for 1 to 2 minutes
   until light and fluffy. Using a rubber spatula, scrape
   the bottom and sides of the bowl. Beat in vanilla. Add
   eggs one at a time, beating for 1 to 2 minutes after each.
   Stir in cooled date mixture and then dry ingredients.
   Combine well.

4. Spoon batter into prepared pan. Using a moistened
   rubber spatula, spread to edges and smooth top. Let stand
   30 minutes.

5. Meanwhile, preheat oven to 350°F (180°C).

6. Bake for 25 to 35 minutes or until a tester inserted in the
   center comes out clean. Let pudding cool in pan on a rack
   for 10 minutes. Remove from pan and serve warm.

Nutrients per serving

Calories	212
Fat	6 g
Saturated fat	4 g
Cholesterol	45 mg
Sodium	169 mg
Carbohydrate	38 g
Fiber	3 g
Protein	3 g
Calcium	28 mg
Iron	1 mg

Toffee Sauce

**Makes 2 cups
(500 mL)
(12 servings)**

This buttery sweet
sauce is best when
served warm. Serve
over Christmas Pudding
(page 202).

Tips

The sauce can be frozen
for up to 2 months. It stays
soft enough to scoop out in
small quantities. Warm in the
microwave on Medium (50%)
for 1 to 2 minutes.

Do not make substitutions
for butter.

⅔ cup	butter	150 mL
⅔ cup	packed brown sugar	150 mL
⅓ cup	liquid honey	75 mL
⅔ cup	2% evaporated milk	150 mL

1. In a small saucepan, combine butter, brown sugar and honey. Heat gently over low heat, stirring constantly, until sugar dissolves. Simmer for 2 to 3 minutes or until sauce thickens and bubbles. Stir in evaporated milk and remove from heat.

Variation

If the sauce is too sweet or too thick for your taste,
increase evaporated milk to 1 cup (250 mL).

Steamed Christmas Pudding: In Step 4, place batter
in a buttered 6½-cup (1.5 L) ceramic mold and cover
tightly with greased foil. Place on a rack in a large
saucepan; add boiling water halfway up the mold.
Turn heat to low, cover and steam over simmering
water for 1½ to 2 hours or until a tester inserted
in the center comes out clean. Add more water as
necessary. The steaming time depends on the shape
of your mold.

Nutrients per serving

Calories	177
Fat	10 g
Saturated fat	6 g
Cholesterol	29 mg
Sodium	21 mg
Carbohydrate	21 g
Fiber	0 g
Protein	1 g
Calcium	49 mg
Iron	0 mg

New York–Style Cheesecake

Makes 12 servings

Choose your favorite GF crust for this recipe: either homemade from shortbread or a commercial one. You can vary it every time to suit your cravings.

Tips

For making almond flour, see Nut flour in Techniques Glossary, page 217.

Ultra-low-fat, fat-free or soft cream cheese cannot be substituted for regular brick cream cheese in baked cheesecake recipes. However, light cream cheese can be used.

If using a dark-colored spring-form pan, decrease the oven temperature by 25°F (10°C).

Leaving the cheesecake in the oven after turning off the oven helps prevent large cracks.

Loosen cake from edges of springform pan before opening the side clip.

Nutrients per serving

Calories	444
Fat	34 g
Saturated fat	18 g
Cholesterol	138 mg
Sodium	286 mg
Carbohydrate	29 g
Fiber	1 g
Protein	7 g
Calcium	96 mg
Iron	1 mg

- Preheat oven to 300°F (150°C)
- 9-inch (23 cm) springform pan
- Electric hand mixer
- Large roasting pan

2 cups	shortbread cookie crumbs (page 146)	500 mL
½ cup	almond flour	125 mL
3 tbsp	butter, melted	45 mL
3	packages (8 oz/250 g) cream cheese, softened	3
¾ cup	granulated sugar	175 mL
1 tbsp	grated lemon zest	15 mL
2 tbsp	freshly squeezed lemon juice	30 mL
3	eggs	3
3 tbsp	amaranth flour	45 mL
1 cup	GF sour cream	250 mL

1. In a medium bowl, combine crumbs and almond flour with butter. Press into bottom of springform pan. Refrigerate for 10 minutes.

2. In a large bowl, using an electric hand mixer, beat cream cheese until smooth. Gradually beat in sugar, lemon zest and lemon juice until light and fluffy. Beat in eggs, one at a time. Stir in amaranth flour and sour cream. Pour into crust.

3. Place springform pan in roasting pan and place in preheated oven. Pour enough hot water into roasting pan to fill it to a depth of at least 1 inch (2.5 cm) up springform pan. Bake for 60 to 75 minutes or until center is just set and the blade of a knife comes out clean.

4. Turn oven off and let cheesecake cool in oven for 30 minutes. Carefully remove springform pan from roasting pan. Using a knife, trace around outside edge of cake to loosen it. Let cool in springform pan on a rack for 30 minutes. Refrigerate until chilled, about 3 hours.

Variations

Cake crumbs can be substituted for shortbread crumbs in the crust.

Serve with fresh peach sauce or other fruits in season.

Doughnuts

Makes 24 donuts (1 per serving)

These old-fashioned cake doughnuts are a treat.

Tips

See the Equipment Glossary, page 209, for more information on doughnut cutters.

Cut as many doughnuts as possible the first time you roll out dough. If dough becomes sticky, return to the refrigerator for a few minutes. Scraps require chilling before they can be rerolled.

Variations

While still warm, dust doughnuts with sifted GF confectioners' (icing) sugar or cinnamon-sugar.

Sour milk can replace buttermilk. To sour milk, add ½ tsp (2 mL) lemon juice to ½ cup (125 mL) milk.

Nutrients per serving

Calories	72
Fat	2 g
Saturated fat	0 g
Cholesterol	8 mg
Sodium	86 mg
Carbohydrate	13 g
Fiber	1 g
Protein	1 g
Calcium	14 mg
Iron	0 mg

- Electric hand mixer
- Deep fryer or large, deep, heavy-bottomed saucepan
- Candy/deep-fry or infrared thermometer
- 2-inch (5 cm) doughnut cutter

½ cup	whole bean flour	125 mL
¼ cup	amaranth flour	60 mL
⅔ cup	cornstarch	150 mL
⅔ cup	tapioca starch	150 mL
2½ tsp	xanthan gum	12 mL
1¼ tsp	baking soda	6 mL
⅛ tsp	salt	0.5 mL
½ tsp	ground cinnamon	2 mL
¼ tsp	ground nutmeg	1 mL
1	egg	1
½ cup	granulated sugar	125 mL
½ cup	buttermilk	125 mL
2 tbsp	vegetable oil	30 mL
¼ tsp	vanilla extract	1 mL
	Vegetable oil for frying	
	Sweet rice flour	

1. In a large bowl or plastic bag, combine whole bean flour, amaranth flour, cornstarch, tapioca starch, xanthan gum, baking soda, salt, cinnamon and nutmeg. Mix well and set aside.

2. In a separate bowl, using electric hand mixer, beat egg, sugar, buttermilk, vegetable oil and vanilla until blended. Add dry ingredients and mix until combined.

3. Divide dough in half. Place each half between two sheets of plastic wrap and pat out to a disc about ½ inch (1 cm) thick. Wrap airtight and refrigerate overnight.

4. Remove one disc of dough from the refrigerator. Place between two clean sheets of plastic wrap and roll out to ¼ inch (0.5 cm) thick. Cut with doughnut cutter, chilling and rerolling scraps. (If dough sticks to cutter, dip cutter into sweet rice flour.)

5. Heat 2 inches (5 cm) vegetable oil in deep fryer or saucepan until thermometer reads 350°F (180°C).

6. Deep-fry doughnuts, a few at a time, for 20 to 30 seconds on each side or until golden-brown. Drain on a plate lined with paper towel. Repeat with remaining dough. Store doughnuts in an airtight container at room temperature for up to 2 days or freeze for up to 2 months.

Lemon Snow with Raspberry Coulis

Makes 4 servings

This airy, light and delicate lemon treat enhanced with slightly sweet raspberry is perfect at the end of a meal.

Tip
Fresh lemon juice, rather than bottled juice, results in a stronger, better-flavored dessert.

Variation
Substitute ¼ cup (60 mL) pasteurized liquid egg whites for raw egg whites.

- Electric hand mixer fitted with wire whisk attachment
- Four ¾-cup (175 mL) ramekins
- Food processor or blender
- Fine-mesh sieve

Lemon Snow

⅔ cup	granulated sugar, divided	150 mL
¼ cup	cornstarch	60 mL
2 tsp	grated lemon zest	10 mL
1⅓ cups	water	325 mL
⅓ cup	freshly squeezed lemon juice	75 mL
3 tbsp	butter	45 mL
2	egg yolks	2
2	egg whites, at room temperature	2
⅛ tsp	cream of tartar	0.5 mL

Raspberry Coulis

1	package (15 oz/425 g) frozen sweetened raspberries, thawed and juice reserved	1

1. *Lemon Snow:* In a medium saucepan, combine ½ cup (125 mL) sugar and cornstarch. Stir in lemon zest and water. Cook over medium heat, stirring constantly, for 5 to 8 minutes or until mixture boils and thickens. Remove from heat and stir in lemon juice and butter.

2. In a small bowl, whisk egg yolks. Gradually add ¼ cup (60 mL) lemon mixture, whisking until blended. Whisk back into lemon mixture. Return to stovetop and simmer, whisking, for 1 minute. Remove from heat and set aside.

3. In a clean bowl, using electric hand mixer, beat egg whites until foamy. Beat in cream of tartar. Continue beating until egg whites form stiff peaks. Gradually beat in 2 tbsp (30 mL) sugar. Continue beating until mixture is very stiff and glossy but not dry. Fold in warm lemon mixture. Pour into ramekins, dividing evenly. Refrigerate for 1 hour or until set.

4. *Raspberry Coulis:* In food processor or blender, purée raspberries with juice. Press through a fine-mesh sieve. Chill. Spoon over lemon snow just before serving.

Nutrients per serving

Calories	278
Fat	11 g
Saturated fat	6 g
Cholesterol	115 mg
Sodium	112 mg
Carbohydrate	43 g
Fiber	0 g
Protein	3 g
Calcium	20 mg
Iron	0 mg

Equipment Glossary

Baguette pan. A metal baking pan divided into two sections shaped like long, thin loaves. The bottom surface may be perforated with small holes to produce a crisp crust and reduce the baking time.

Cooling rack. A kitchen tool with parallel and perpendicular thin bars at right angles, with feet attached, that is used to hold hot baked goods off surfaces to allow cooling air to circulate.

Crêpe pan. A smooth, low, round pan with a heavy bottom and sloping sides. Crêpe pans range from 5 to 7 inches (12.5 to 18 cm) in diameter.

Doughnut cutters. A utensil made of two 1-inch-high (2.5 cm) rings, the smaller one centered inside the larger one. A U-shaped handle holds the rings together.

Dutch oven. A large, deep pot with a tight-fitting lid, used for stewing and braising.

Fine-mesh sieve. A sieve separates out unwanted material and breaks up clumps in dry ingredients. It also aerates and combines. A sieve is made in a bowl shape, with metal or plastic mesh and a handle of metal or rubber. The size of the holes in the mesh varies depending on use.

English muffin rings. Available in sets of four or eight, 3¾ (9.5 cm) round and 1 inch (2.5 cm) high, these rings hold batter in place as it bakes.

Griddle. A flat metal surface on which food is cooked. It can be built into a stove or stand alone.

Instant-read thermometer. See page 22.

Loaf pan. A container used to bake loaves. Common pan sizes are 8 by 4 inches (20 by 10 cm) and 9 by 5 inches (23 by 12.5 cm).

Mixers. A hand mixer can also be referred to as an electric hand mixer. It is a portable, handheld mixer used for lighter-weight tasks. It has several speeds to use for different operations, from stirring, folding and creaming to kneading and beating. Attachments vary and can include regular flat beaters, softscrape beaters, straight wire beaters, a wire whisk or dough hooks. A hand mixer can be used in any bowl for a quick, easy cleanup. It's also less expensive to purchase than a stand mixer. A stand mixer can also be referred to as a heavy-duty mixer. It allows for hands-free operation, is larger in size and has a more powerful motor than a hand mixer since it's meant for heavy operations such as beating thicker batters and doughs for longer times, as well as for kneading. The various attachments include a flat-coated beater (paddle), dough hook, wire whisk and pouring shield. The metal bowl is removable.

Parchment paper. This heat-resistant paper is similar to waxed paper and is usually coated with silicone on one side. It is used with or as an alternative to other methods (such as applying vegetable oil or spray) to prevent baked goods from sticking to the baking pan. Parchment paper is sometimes labeled "baking paper."

Pastry blender. A tool used to cut solid fat into flour. It consists of five or six metal blades or wires held together by a handle.

Pastry brush. A small brush with nylon or natural bristles used to apply glazes or egg washes to dough. Make sure to wash thoroughly after each use. To store, lay flat or hang on a hook through the hole in the handle.

Pizza wheel. A sharp-edged wheel (without serrations) anchored to a handle.

Portion scoop. A utensil similar to an ice cream scoop, used to measure equal amounts of batter. Cookie scoops come in different sizes, for 2-inch (5 cm), $2\frac{1}{2}$-inch (6 cm) and $3\frac{1}{4}$-inch (8 cm) cookies. Muffin scoops have a $\frac{1}{4}$-cup (60 mL) capacity.

Potato masher. A tool with a handle and head used to crush soft food such as cooked potatoes, turnip or apples. The head can be of different designs, from a rounded zigzag to a plate with holes or slits.

Ramekins. Usually sold as a set of small, deep, straight-sided ceramic soufflé dishes, these are also known as mini bakers. They are used to bake individual servings of a pudding, cobbler or custard. Capacity ranges from 4 oz, or $\frac{1}{2}$ cup (125 mL), to 10 oz, or $1\frac{1}{4}$ cups (300 mL).

Rolling pin. A smooth cylinder of wood, marble, plastic or metal, used to roll out dough.

Slotted spoon. A spoon that has openings in the bowl and can be any size. The function is similar to a sieve. It is used to remove solids from a liquid; for example, removing french fries from the fat.

Soufflé dish. A round, porcelain dish with a ridged exterior and a straight, smooth interior.

Spatula. A utensil with a handle and a blade that can be long or short, narrow or wide, flexible or inflexible. It is used to spread, lift, turn, mix or smooth foods. Spatulas are made of metal, rubber, plastic or silicone.

Springform pan. A circular baking pan, available in a range of sizes, with a separable bottom and side. The side is removed by releasing a clamp, making the contents easy to serve.

Tester. A thin, long wooden or metal stick or wire attached to a handle, used to test for doneness in baked products.

Thermometers.
Instant-read thermometer. See page 22.

Oven thermometer. A thermometer that is used to measure temperatures from 200°F to 500°F (100°C to 260°C). It either stands on or hangs from an oven rack.

Candy/Deep-Fry Thermometer. A thermometer used for testing the temperature during deep frying temperatures ranging from 100°F to 400°F (38°C to 200°C). Look for one with a handle, adjustable hooks or clips to attach it to a pan and hold it in place. There are dual-purpose thermometers with readings both for candy and deep fat.

Waffle maker. A small electric appliance with two hinged indented plates that make a grid pattern, becoming small recesses in the waffle for filling with butter and/or syrup.

Zester. A tool used to cut very thin strips of outer peel from citrus fruits. One type has a short, flat blade tipped with five small holes with sharp edges. Another popular style is made of stainless steel and looks like a tool used for planing wood in a workshop.

Ingredient Glossary

Almonds. Crack open the shell of an almond and you will find an ivory-colored nut encased in a thin, brown skin. With the skin on, almonds are called natural. With the skin removed (see Techniques Glossary, page 216), almonds are called blanched. In this form, almonds are sold whole, sliced, slivered and ground. Two cups (500 mL) almonds weigh 12 oz (375 g). Sweet almonds have a delicate taste that is delicious in breads, cookies, cakes, fillings and candies. Both blanched and natural are interchangeable in recipes.

Almond flour (almond meal). See page 14.

Amaranth flour. See page 9.

Apricots. A small stone fruit with a thin, pale yellow to orange skin and a meaty orange flesh. Dried unpeeled apricot halves are used in baking.

Arrowroot. See page 15.

Asiago cheese. A pungent, grayish-white hard cheese from northern Italy. Cured for more than 6 months, its texture is ideal for grating.

Baking powder. A chemical leavener containing an alkali (baking soda) and an acid (cream of tartar) that gives off carbon dioxide gas under certain conditions. Make sure to select gluten-free baking powder.

Baking soda (sodium bicarbonate). A chemical leavener that gives off carbon dioxide gas in the presence of moisture — particularly acids such as lemon juice, buttermilk and sour cream. It is also one of the components of baking powder.

Balsamic vinegar. A dark Italian vinegar made from grape juice that has been cooked until the water content is reduced by half, then it is aged for several years in wooden barrels. It has a pungent sweetness and can be used to make salad dressings and marinades or drizzled over roasted or grilled vegetables.

Bean flours. See Legume Flours, page 13.

Bell peppers. These sweet-flavored members of the capsicum family (which includes chiles and other hot peppers) have a hollow interior lined with white ribs and seeds attached at the stem end. They are most commonly green, red, orange or yellow, but they can also be white or purple.

Blueberries. Wild low-bush berries are smaller than the cultivated variety and more time-consuming to pick, but their flavor makes every minute of picking time worthwhile. They are readily available year-round in the frozen fruit section of most grocery stores.

Brown rice flour. See page 10.

Buckwheat. See page 9.

Butter. A spread produced from dairy fat and milk solids, butter is interchangeable with shortening, oil or margarine in most recipes.

Buttermilk. Named for the way it was originally produced — that is, from milk left in the churn after the solid butter was removed — buttermilk now is made with fresh, pasteurized milk that has been cultured (or soured) with the addition of a bacterial culture. The result is a slightly thickened dairy beverage with a salty, sour flavor similar to yogurt. Despite its name, buttermilk is low in fat. It is also available in a powder form.

The powder is low in calories, softening the textures of breads and heightening the flavors of ingredients such as chocolate. It is readily available at bulk or health food stores. Store in an airtight container, as it lumps easily. To substitute for 1 cup (250 ml) fresh buttermilk, use 1 cup (250 mL) water and $\frac{1}{3}$ cup (75 mL) buttermilk powder. If unavailable, substitute an equal amount of skim milk powder.

Candied pineapple. Fresh pineapple that has been preserved in sugar. Soak fresh fruit pieces in a sugar syrup, then heat mixture until all of the fruit's original water content is replaced with sugar. It can be served as is, added to recipes or used as a garnish. Store at room temperature — it has a long shelf life.

Cardamom. This popular spice is a member of the ginger family. A long green or brown pod contains the strong, spicy, lemon-flavored seed.

Cassava. A plant that originates from South America from which tapioca is extracted.

Cheddar cheese. Always select an aged, good-quality Cheddar for baking recipes. The flavor of mild or medium Cheddar is not strong enough for baking.

Chickpea (garbanzo bean) flour. See page 13.

Confectioners' sugar (also called icing sugar, powdered fondant). White sugar that has been ground to a fine powder, then sifted. It usually contains 3% cornstarch as an anticaking agent, to prevent clumping. It is used in icing confections and whipped cream. Canadian icing sugar may contain wheat starch, so check the label. Always sift confectioners' sugar right before using.

Cornmeal/corn flour. See page 9.

Cornstarch. See page 15.

Cranberries. Grown in bogs on low vines, these sweet-tart berries are available fresh, frozen and dried. Fresh cranberries are available only in season — typically from mid-October until January, depending on your location — but can be frozen right in the bag. Substitute dried cranberries for sour cherries, raisins or currants.

Cream of tartar. Used to give volume and stability to beaten egg whites, cream of tartar is also an acidic component of baking powder. Tartaric acid is a fine, white crystalline powder that forms naturally during the fermentation of grape juice on the inside of wine barrels.

Cross-contamination. The process by which one product comes in contact with another that is to be avoided. For example, toasters, oven mitts, cutting boards and knives, when used for products containing gluten, still have gluten on them, which is passed on to the gluten-free product. You must either have separate tools or be sure that the gluten is washed off completely before the tools are used by people with gluten sensitivity.

Dates. The fruit of the date palm tree, dates are long and oval in shape, with a paper-thin skin that turns from green to dark brown when ripe. Eaten fresh or dried, dates have a very sweet, light brown flesh around a long, narrow seed.

Eggs. Liquid egg products, such as Naturegg Simply Egg Whites, Break-Free and Omega Plus liquid eggs and Just Whites, are available in the United States and Canada. Powdered egg whites, such as Just Whites, can be used as a powder or by reconstituting them with warm water. A similar product is called meringue powder in Canada. Substitute 2 tbsp (30 mL) liquid egg product for each white of a large egg.

Fava bean flour. See page 13.

Feta cheese. A crumbly and white Greek-style cheese with a salty, tangy flavor. Store in the refrigerator, in its brine, and drain well before using. It is traditionally made with sheep's or goat's milk in Greece and usually with cow's milk in the United States and Canada.

Filberts. See Hazelnuts.

Flax seeds. See page 13.

Garbanzo bean (chickpea) flour. See page 13.

Garfava (garbanzo-fava bean) flour. See page 13.

Garlic. An edible bulb composed of several sections (cloves), each covered with a papery skin. An essential ingredient in many styles of cooking.

Ginger. Fresh gingerroot is a bumpy rhizome, ivory to greenish yellow in color, with a tan skin. It has a peppery, slightly sweet flavor, similar to lemon and rosemary, and a pungent aroma. Ground ginger is made from dried gingerroot. It is spicier and not as sweet or as fresh. Crystallized, or candied, ginger is made from pieces of fresh gingerroot that have been cooked in sugar syrup and coated with sugar.

Glacé cherries. Maraschino cherries with the pit removed that are then candied in sugar syrup. They are very sweet.

Gluten. A natural protein in wheat flour that becomes elastic with the addition of moisture and kneading. Gluten traps gases produced by leaveners inside the dough and causes it to rise.

Glutinous rice flour. See Sweet rice flour, page 215.

Granulated sugar. Normal white table sugar, made from beetroot or sugarcane. The crystals vary in size.

Guar gum. A white, flour-like substance made from an East Indian seed high in fiber, this vegetable substance contains no gluten. However, it can have a laxative effect for some people. It can be substituted for xanthan gum.

Half-and-half cream. The lightest of all the creams, it is half milk, half cream and has a butterfat content between 10% and 18%. It can't be whipped, but it is used with coffee or on cereal. To substitute, use equal parts cream and milk or evaporated milk or $\frac{7}{8}$ cup (210 mL) milk, plus $1\frac{1}{2}$ tbsp (22 mL) butter or margarine.

Hazelnut flour (hazelnut meal). See page 14.

Hazelnuts. Slightly larger than filberts, hazelnuts have a weaker flavor. Both nuts have a round, smooth shell and look like small, brown marbles. They have a sweet, rich flavor and are interchangeable in recipes.

Herbs. Edible plants whose stems, leaves or flowers are used as a flavoring, either dried or fresh. To substitute fresh herbs for dried, a good rule of thumb is to use three times the amount of fresh as dried. Taste and adjust the amount to suit your preference.

Legume flours. See page 13.

Linseed. See flax seeds, page 13.

Maple syrup. A very sweet, slightly thick brown liquid made by boiling the sap from North American maple trees. Use pure maple syrup, not pancake syrup, in baking.

Margarine. A solid fat derived from one or more types of vegetable oil. Do not use lower-fat margarines in baking because they contain too much added water.

Millet. See page 10.

Mixed candied fruit. A mixture of orange and lemon peel, citron and glazed cherries. Mixed candied peel includes orange, lemon and citron peel. Expensive citron may be replaced by candied rutabaga.

Molasses. A by-product of refining sugar, molasses is a sweet, thick, dark brown (almost black) liquid. It has a distinctive, slightly bitter flavor and is available in fancy and blackstrap varieties. Use the fancy version for baking unless blackstrap is specified. Store in the refrigerator if used infrequently.

Nonfat dry milk. See Skim milk powder.

Nut flours (nut meals). See page 14.

Oats. See page 9.

Olive oil. An oil produced from pressing tree-ripened olives. Extra virgin oil is taken from the first cold pressing; it is the finest and fruitiest, pale straw to pale green in color, with the least amount of acid, usually less than 1%. Virgin oil is taken from a subsequent pressing; it contains 2% acid and is pale yellow. Light oil comes from the last pressing; it has a mild flavor, light color and up to 3% acid. It also has a higher smoke point. Product sold as "pure olive oil" has been cleaned and filtered; it is very mild-flavored and has up to 3% acid.

Olives, kalamata. A large, flavorful variety of Greek olive, typically dark purple in color and pointed at one end.

Pea flours. See page 14.

Pecan flour (pecan meal). See page 14.

Pecans. This sweet, mellow nut is smooth and oval, golden brown on the outside and tan on the inside. You can purchase pecans whole, halved, chopped or in chips.

Peel (mixed candied). Peel is made from the outside skin of orange, lemon, lime or grapefruit, which is then cut into strips. To make mixed candied peel, cook a mixture of citrus peel in water first and then a sugar syrup.

Peppers. See Bell peppers.

Potato starch (potato starch flour) See page 15.

Provolone cheese. An Italian cheese with a light ivory color, mild mellow flavor and smooth texture that cuts without crumbling. Available shapes are sausage, squat pear and piglet.

Pumpkin seeds. These seeds are available roasted or raw, salted or unsalted and with or without hulls. Raw pumpkin seeds without hulls — often known as pepitas ("little seeds" in Spanish) — are a dull, dark olive green. Roasted pumpkin seeds have a rich, almost peanuty flavor.

Quinoa. See page 10.

Raisins. Dark raisins are sun-dried Thompson seedless grapes that have been dried naturally. Sultana or golden raisins are dried white seedless grapes varieties. Golden in color and plumper, sweeter and juicier than other raisins, they are treated with sulfur dioxide and dried artificially.

Rhubarb. A perennial plant with long, thin red- to pink-colored stalks resembling celery and large, green leaves. Only the tart-flavored stalks are used for cooking because the leaves are poisonous. For 2 cups (500 mL) cooked rhubarb, you will need 3 cups (750 mL) chopped fresh (about 1 lb/500 g).

Rice bran and rice polish. See page 10.

Rice flours. See page 10.

Sesame seeds. These small, flat oval seeds, which can be ivory, red, brown, pale gold or black, have a nutty, slightly sweet flavor. Purchase the tan (hulled), not black (unhulled), variety for use in baking. Black sesame seeds have a more pungent flavor and bitter taste than white or natural sesame seeds.

Shortening. A partially hydrogenated, solid, white flavorless fat made from vegetable sources.

Skim milk powder. This milk is the dehydrated form of fluid skim milk. Use 1/4 cup (60 mL) skim milk powder for every 1 cup (250 mL) water.

Sorghum flour. See page 10.

Sour cream. This is a thick, smooth, tangy product made by adding bacterial cultures to pasteurized, homogenized cream that contains varying amounts of butterfat. Check the label: some lower-fat and fat-free brands may contain gluten.

Soy flour. See page 14.

Starches. See page 15.

Sun-dried tomatoes. Available either dry or packed in oil, sun-dried tomatoes have a dark red color, a soft chewy texture and a strong tomato flavor. Use dry-packed, not oil-packed, sun-dried tomatoes in our recipes. Use scissors to snip the ends. Oil-packed and dry-packed are not interchangeable in recipes.

Sunflower seeds. These plump, nut-like kernels grow in teardrop shapes within gray-and-white shells. They are sold raw or roasted and salted, seasoned or plain. Shelled sunflower seeds are sometimes labeled "sunflower kernels" or "nutmeats." When buying seeds in the shell, look for clean, unbroken shells. Use shelled, unsalted, unroasted sunflower seeds in bread recipes. If only roasted, salted seeds are available, rinse under hot water and dry well before using.

Superfine sugar. Also known as bar, berry or caster sugar, superfine sugar is sugar that has been ground into finer crystals than regular granulated white sugar. It resembles sand in an hourglass and is not as fine as powdered confectioners' (icing) sugar. It is popular with bakers because the smaller crystals cream very easily into butter and dissolve more readily into meringues and batters, producing a finer crumb and a lighter texture when finished.

Sweet peppers. See Bell peppers.

Sweet rice flour. See page 10.

Tapioca starch. See page 15.

Teff. See page 12.

Vegetable oil. Common vegetable oils are canola, corn, sunflower, safflower, olive, peanut and soy.

Walnuts. Inside a tough shell, a walnut's curly nutmeat halves offer a rich, sweet flavor, and the edible, papery skin adds a hint of bitterness to baked goods. Walnuts are available whole (shelled and unshelled), halved and chopped.

Whole bean flour. See page 13.

Wild rice. This is not actually a rice but a marsh grass seed with long, shiny black or dark brown grains. Because of its rich, roasted, smoky, nutty flavor and chewy texture, wild rice complements wild game, poultry and berries.

Xanthan gum. See page 15.

Yeast. See page 17.

Yogurt. This is a food made by fermenting cow's milk using a bacteria culture. Plain yogurt is gluten-free, but not all flavored yogurt is, so be sure to check labels.

Zest. Used for its intense flavor, zest is stripped from the outer layer of rind (the colored part only) of citrus fruit. Avoid the bitter part underneath (called the pith).

Techniques Glossary

Almond flour (almond meal). *To make:* See Nut flour. *To toast:* Spread in a 9-inch (23 cm) baking pan and bake at 350°F (180°C), stirring occasionally, for 8 minutes or until light golden.

Almonds. *To blanch:* Cover almonds with boiling water and let stand, covered, for 3 to 5 minutes. Drain. Grasp the almond at one end, pressing between your thumb and index finger, and the nut will pop out of the skin. Nuts are more easily chopped or slivered while still warm from blanching. *To toast:* see Nuts.

Bananas. *To mash and freeze:* Select overripe fruit, mash and package in 1 cup (250 mL) amounts in freezer containers. Freeze for up to 6 months. Defrost and warm to room temperature before using. Two to 3 medium bananas yield 1 cup (250 mL) mashed.

Beat. To stir vigorously to incorporate air, using a spoon, whisk, handheld beater or electric mixer.

Blend. To mix two or more ingredients together thoroughly, with a spoon or using the low speed of an electric mixer.

Bread crumbs. *To make fresh:* For best results, GF bread should be at least one day old. Using the pulsing option of a food processor or blender, process until crumbs are of the desired consistency. *To make dry:* Spread bread crumbs in a single layer on a baking sheet and bake at 350°F (180°C) for 6 to 8 minutes, shaking pan frequently, until lightly browned, crisp and dry. (Or microwave, uncovered, on High for 1 to 2 minutes, stirring every 30 seconds.) *To store:* Package in airtight containers and freeze for up to 3 months.

Butterfly. To split food through the middle of the thickness without completely separating the halves, then spreading halves to resemble a butterfly or the open pages of a book.

Examples are shrimp, steak, chicken breast or pork chop. The food cooks more quickly and evenly because twice as much surface area is exposed to heat.

Cake crumbs. See Bread crumbs.

Chocolate. *To melt:* Foods high in fat, such as chocolate, soften and then become a liquid when heated. Microwave on Medium (50%) for 1 minute per 1-oz (30 g) square or until soft. Stir until completely melted.

Combine. To stir two or more ingredients together for a consistent mixture.

Cream. To combine softened fat and sugar by beating to a soft, smooth, creamy consistency, while trying to incorporate as much air as possible.

Cut in. To combine solid fat and flour until the fat is the size required (for example, the size of small peas or meal). Use either two knives or a pastry blender.

Difference between chop and dice. *Chop* is a cutting technique that involves cutting food into larger, irregular, non-uniform-shaped pieces. *Dice* is a cutting technique that involves cutting food into smaller, uniform, cube-shaped pieces. It is more time consuming.

Drizzle. To slowly spoon or pour a liquid (such as frosting or melted butter) in a very fine stream over the surface of food.

Dust. Coating by sprinkling GF confectioners' (icing) sugar, cocoa powder or any GF flour lightly over food or a utensil.

Eggs. *To warm to room temperature:* Place eggs in the shell from the refrigerator in a bowl of hot water and let stand for 5 minutes.

Egg whites. *To warm to room temperature:* Separate eggs while cold. Place bowl of egg whites in a larger bowl filled with hot water and let stand for 5 minutes. *To beat to soft peaks:* Beat to a thickness that comes up as beaters are lifted and folds over at the tips. *To beat to stiff peaks:* Beat past soft peaks until the peaks remain upright when beaters are lifted.

Egg yolks. *To warm to room temperature:* Separate eggs while cold. Place bowl of egg yolks in a larger bowl filled with hot water and let stand for 5 minutes.

Flax seeds. *To grind:* Place whole seeds in a coffee grinder or blender. Grind only the amount required. If necessary, store extra ground flax seeds in the refrigerator. *To crack:* Pulse in a coffee grinder, blender or food processor just long enough to break the seed coat, but not long enough to grind completely.

Fold. Folding gently combines light, whipped ingredients with heavier ingredients without losing the incorporated air. Using a rubber spatula, gently fold in a circular motion. Move down one side of the bowl and across the bottom. Fold up and over to the opposite inside and down again, turning bowl slightly after each fold.

Garlic. *To peel:* Use the flat side of a sharp knife to flatten garlic clove. Skin can then be easily removed.

Griddle. To test for correct temperature, see Skillet.

Grease baking pan. *To prepare or to grease:* Either spray the bottom and sides of the baking pan with GF nonstick cooking spray or brush with a pastry brush or a crumpled-up piece of waxed paper dipped in vegetable oil or shortening.

Hazelnut flour (hazelnut meal). *To make:* See Nut flour. *To toast:* Spread in a 9-inch (23 cm) baking pan and bake at 350°F (180°C), stirring occasionally, for 8 minutes or until light golden. Let cool before using.

Instant-read thermometer. *To test baked goods for doneness:* See page 22.

Line pan. Pans can be lined with parchment paper, waxed paper or heavy brown paper. A recipe will state whether you are lining only the bottom of the pan or the sides and bottom. Trace the outline of the pan on paper, then cut it out with scissors. Place paper with clean side up (and the side used for tracing down). Heavy brown paper prevents batters that are baked for a long period of time from browning too quickly. Heavy brown paper bags are found in grocery stores or sheets of brown wrapping paper can be used. Post offices also have heavy brown wrapping paper.

Mix. To mix means to combine two or more ingredients uniformly by stirring or using an electric mixer on a low speed.

Nut flour (nut meal). *To make:* Toast nuts (see Nuts). Let cool to room temperature and grind in a food processor or blender to desired consistency. *To make using ground nuts:* Bake at 350°F (180°C) for 6 to 8 minutes, let cool to room temperature and grind to a finer consistency.

Nuts. *To toast:* Spread nuts in a single layer on a baking sheet and bake at 350°F (180°C) for 6 to 8 minutes, shaking baking sheet frequently, until fragrant and lightly browned. (Or microwave, uncovered, on High, for 1 to 2 minutes, stirring every 30 seconds.) Nuts will darken upon cooling.

Pecan flour (pecan meal). *To make:* See Nut flour.

Sauté. To cook quickly at a high temperature in a small amount of fat.

Skillet. *To test for correct temperature:* Sprinkle a few drops of water on the surface of the pan.

If the water bounces and dances across the pan, it is ready to use. If the drops of water evaporate, it is too hot.

Stir in. To gently incorporate additional ingredients into an existing mixture. This can be done with an electric mixer on low speed or by hand, using a spoon or a spatula.

Roux. The technique of making a roux is the first step of a basic white sauce. Equal parts flour and butter are cooked to use as a thickener for sauces and soups. Because the flour is coated with fat, it lets you mix with a liquid to thicken a sauce base without the flour forming lumps.

Temporary emulsion. Oil and vinegar don't mix. Whisking and/or shaking will cause them to stay together for a short time. This is called a temporary emulsion. Both Dijon mustard and honey act as stabilizers during this process.

Tent with foil. When you want to prevent further browning in the oven, place a sheet of aluminum foil lightly over pan to make a tent. Place foil shiny side up. Do not tuck foil around pan, which allows hot air to circulate underneath.

Trussing. To tie down the legs and wings of poultry, ensuring they don't flop around during the cooking process. It helps the poultry cook more evenly, so that the white and dark meat finish cooking at the same time.

Waffle maker. To test for correct temperature, see Skillet.

Wild rice. *To cook:* Rinse 1 cup (250 mL) wild rice under cold running water. Add along with 6 cups (1.5 L) water to a large saucepan. Bring to a boil and cook, uncovered, at a gentle boil for about 35 minutes. Reduce heat, cover and cook for 10 minutes or until rice is soft but not mushy. Makes 3 cups (750 mL). Store in refrigerator for up to 1 week.

Yeast. *To test for freshness:* See page 17.

Zest. *To zest:* Use a zester, the fine side of a box grater or a small, sharp knife to peel off thin strips of the colored part of the skin of citrus fruits. Be sure not to remove the bitter white pith below.

About the Nutrient Analysis

The nutrient analysis done on the recipes in this book was derived from the Food Processor SQL Nutrition Analysis Software, version 10.9, ESHA Research (2011).

Where necessary, data was supplemented using the following references: USDA National Nutrient Database for Standard Reference, Release #28 (2016). Retrieved April 2017, from the USDA Agricultural Research Service website: www.nal.usda.gov/fnic/foodcomp/search/.

Recipes were evaluated as follows:

- The larger number of servings was used where there is a range.

- Where alternatives are given, the first ingredient and amount listed were used.

- Optional ingredients and ingredients that are not quantified were not included.

- Calculations were based on imperial measures and weights.

- Nutrient values were rounded to the nearest whole number.

- The smaller quantity of an ingredient was used where a range is provided.

- Canola oil was used where the ingredient is listed as vegetable oil.

- Milk 1%, salted butter, and large eggs were used where the ingredient is listed as milk, butter, and eggs respectively.

- Regular-fat products were used for sour cream, cream cheese and cheese.

- Recipes were analyzed prior to cooking.

It is important to note that the cooking method used to prepare the recipe may alter the nutrient content per serving, as may ingredient substitutions and differences among brand-name products.

Index

A

All-Dressed Pizza, Traditional, 52
almonds, 211, 216
  Almond Biscotti, 142
  Almond Pound Cake, 159
  Fruitcake, 164
almond flour/meal, 14, 21, 216
  Cheese Biscuits Two Ways, 130
  Cinnamon Raisin Bread, 110
  Coconut Shrimp, 84
  Cottage Pudding with Brown
    Sugar Sauce, 162
  Dinner Rolls, 97
  German Christmas Stollen, 112
  Irish Soda Bread, 136
  Nanaimo Bars (variation), 150
  New York–Style Cheesecake,
    204
  Raspberry Breakfast Danish, 114
  Raspberry Jelly Roll, 168
  Sponge Cake, 174
  Strawberry Shortcake, 128
  Stuffing Bread, 98
  White Bread, 96
  White Cake, 175
amaranth flour, 9, 16, 21
  Almond Biscotti, 142
  Almond Pound Cake, 159
  Apple Crumble Pie, 184
  Blueberry Hazelnut Crumble
    Coffee Cake, 166
  Buttermilk Scones, 134
  Cinnamon Raisin Bread, 110
  Cornbread, 132
  Cottage Pudding with Brown
    Sugar Sauce, 162
  Cream Sauce, 91
  Crêpes, 196
  Date Nut Loaf, 126
  Date Squares, 151
  Dinner Rolls, 97
  Doughnuts, 206
  Focaccia, 104
  Frosted Carrot Cake, 160
  Lemon Squares, 152
  Peanut Butter Chunk Cookies,
    148
  Raspberry Breakfast Danish,
    114
  Sponge Cake, 174
  Stuffing Bread, 98
  Turkey Gravy (variation), 75
  White Bread, 96
  White Cake, 175
apples and applesauce
  Apple Crisp, 194
  Apple Crumble Pie, 184
  Raspberry Breakfast Danish
    (variation), 114
arrowroot, 15, 16

B

Bacon
  Buckwheat Pancakes with
    Mixed Grill, 44
  Caesar Salad with Dijon
    Dressing, 36
  Cheese Biscuits Two Ways
    (variation), 130
  Chicken Fingers (variation), 78
  Cornbread (variation), 132
  New England Clam Chowder,
    34
  Quiche Lorraine, 87
baking
  equipment, 209–10
  ingredients, 13–19, 211–15
  techniques, 216–18
bananas, 216
  Banana Bread, 124
  Banana Chocolate Chip
    Muffins, 120
bars and squares, 150–54
  baking tips, 140–41
Basic Rich Biscuits, 127
beans. See bean flour; legumes
bean flour, 13
  Carrot Raisin Muffins, 122
  Chocolate Chip Cookies, 147
  Doughnuts, 206
  Ginger Snaps, 144
  Hearty Beef Stew with Biscuit
    Topping, 62
  Mock Date Bran Muffins, 123
  Red Velvet Cake, 172
  Thin Pizza Crust Two Ways,
    Classic, 48
beef
  Hearty Beef Stew with Biscuit
    Topping, 62
  Lasagna, 58
  Microwave Meatloaf, 61
  Spaghetti and Meatballs, 56
  Tacos, 68
  Tourtière, 66
berries
  Almond Biscotti (variation),
    142
  Blueberry Hazelnut Crumble
    Coffee Cake, 166
  Buttermilk Waffles, Classic
    (variation), 46
  Lemon Snow with Raspberry
    Coulis, 208
  Raspberry Pecan Vinaigrette,
    41
  Strawberry Shortcake, 128
biscuits and scones, 127–30, 134
  baking tips, 119
blueberries, 211. See also berries
Blue Cheese Dressing, 40
bran, 8, 10
  Brown Sandwich Bread, 100
  Mock Date Bran Muffins, 123
  Mock Pumpernickel Loaf, 101
brandy and rum
  Cottage Pudding with Brown
    Sugar Sauce (variation), 162
  Crêpes Suzette, 198
  Pecan Pie (variation), 190
bread crumbs, 216
breads, quick, 124–36
  baking tips, 118
breads, yeast, 93–114
  baking methods, 94–95
bread (as ingredient)
  French Onion Soup, Classic, 33
  Garlic Croutons, 37
  Poultry Stuffing, 74
broccoli
  Broccoli and Cheese Soup, 29
  Cornbread (variation), 132
  Quiche Lorraine (variation), 87
  Vegetarian Pizza, 50
Brownies, Fudgy, 154
Brown Sandwich Bread, 100
buckwheat, 9, 21
  Buckwheat Pancakes with
    Mixed Grill, 44
  Date Squares (variation), 151

buttermilk, 211
  Buckwheat Pancakes with
    Mixed Grill, 44
  Buttermilk Scones, 134
  Classic Buttermilk Waffles, 46
  Cornbread, 132
  Doughnuts, 206
  German Chocolate Cake, 170
  Mock Date Bran Muffins, 123
  Red Velvet Cake, 172
Butter Tarts, 186

C

Caesar Salad with Dijon Dressing,
  36
cakes, 159–75
  baking tips, 158
  frostings, 173
calcium, 20
carbohydrates, 20
carrots
  Broccoli and Cheese Soup, 29
  Carrot Raisin Muffins, 122
  Chicken Noodle Soup, 30
  Chicken Pot Pie, 76
  Frosted Carrot Cake, 160
celery
  Chicken Noodle Soup, 30
  Pasta Salad, 38
  Poultry Stuffing, 74
  Salmon Patties, 82
cheese, 212. See also cream cheese
  All-Dressed Pizza, Traditional,
    52
  Blue Cheese Dressing, 40
  Broccoli and Cheese Soup, 29
  Caesar Salad with Dijon
    Dressing, 36
  Cheese Biscuits Two Ways, 130
  Cheese Sauce for Veggies, 90
  Cheese Soufflé, 60
  Chicken Fingers (variation), 78
  Cornbread (variation), 132
  Crusty French Baguette
    (variation), 102
  French Onion Soup, Classic, 33
  Hawaiian Pizza, 53
  Lasagna, 58
  Mac 'n' Cheese, 54
  Mediterranean Focaccia
    Topping, 106
  Pasta Salad, 38
  Quiche Lorraine, 87
  Triple-Cheese Focaccia
    Topping, 105

Veal Parmesan, 64
Vegetarian Pizza, 50
cherries, 213
  Almond Biscotti (variation),
    142
  Fruitcake, 164
chicken and turkey
  Chicken Fingers, 78
  Chicken Noodle Soup, 30
  Chicken Pot Pie, 76
  Hawaiian Pizza (variation), 53
  Oven-Fried Chicken, 70
  Roast Turkey, 72
  Spaghetti and Meatballs, 56
chickpea flour, 13
chocolate, 216. See also cocoa
  powder
  Banana Chocolate Chip
    Muffins, 120
  Butter Tarts (variation), 186
  Chocolate Chip Cookies, 147
  Fudgy Brownies, 154
  German Chocolate Cake, 170
  Nanaimo Bars, 150
  Raspberry Jelly Roll (variation),
    168
Christmas Pudding, 202
Cinnamon Raisin Bread, 110
Classic Buttermilk Waffles, 46
Classic French Onion Soup, 33
Classic Pastry Two Ways, 180
Classic Thin Pizza Crust Two
  Ways, 48
cocoa powder. See also chocolate
  Chocolate Pudding Cake, 200
  Crêpes (variation), 196
  Red Velvet Cake, 172
coconut
  Coconut Shrimp, 84
  Nanaimo Bars, 150
cookies, 142–48
  baking tips, 140–41
cooking. See baking
cornmeal, 9, 21
  Chicken Fingers, 78
  Cornbread, 132
  Veal Parmesan, 64
cornstarch, 15, 16, 21
  Classic Pastry Two Ways, 180
  Doughnuts, 206
  Lemon Squares, 152
  Pecan Pastry Two Ways, 182
Cottage Pudding with Brown
  Sugar Sauce, 162
cranberries, 212. See also berries

cream cheese
  Cream Cheese Frosting, 173
  New York–Style Cheesecake,
    204
  Raspberry Breakfast Danish, 114
Cream of Mushroom Soup, 32
Cream Sauce, 91
Creamy Rice Pudding, 199
Crêpes, 196
Crêpes Suzette, 198
Crusty French Baguette, 102

D

dates, 212
  Christmas Pudding, 202
  Creamy Rice Pudding
    (variation), 199
  Date Nut Loaf, 126
  Date Squares, 151
  Mock Date Bran Muffins, 123
Dinner Rolls, 97
Doughnuts, 206

E

eggs, 212, 216–17
  Cheese Soufflé, 60
  Lemon Meringue Pie, 188
  Quiche Lorraine, 87
  Salmon Patties, 82
  Sponge Cake, 174
endosperm, 8

F

fat, 13, 20, 178
fava bean flour, 13
fiber, 20
fish and seafood
  Coconut Shrimp, 84
  Fish and Chips, 80
  New England Clam Chowder,
    34
  Quiche Lorraine (variation), 87
  Salmon Patties, 82
  Seafood Fettuccine, 86
flax seeds, 13, 19, 217
  Cinnamon Raisin Bread
    (variation), 110
flours. See also specific types of flour
  nutrient content, 20–21
  storing, 12, 19
Focaccia, 104
Focaccia Topping, Mediterranean,
  106
Focaccia Topping, Triple-Cheese,
  105

French Baguette, Crusty, 102
French Onion Soup, Classic, 33
Frosted Carrot Cake, 160
frostings, 173
fruit, candied, 212, 213
    Fruitcake, 164
    German Christmas Stollen, 112
fruit, dried, 211, 212. *See also* dates;
    raisins
    Almond Biscotti (variation), 142
Fudgy Brownies, 154

G

Galette, 183
garfava flour, 13, 21
garlic, 213, 217
    Crusty French Baguette
        (variation), 102
    Garlic Croutons, 37
    Triple-Cheese Focaccia
        Topping, 105
germ, 8
German Chocolate Cake, 170
German Christmas Stollen, 112
gingerroot, 213
    Ginger Snaps, 144
gluten, 213
grains (whole), 8–12
    gluten-free, 9–12
    nutrient content, 20–21
greens
    Caesar Salad with Dijon
        Dressing, 36
    Chicken Fingers (variation), 78
    Lasagna, 58
    Pasta Salad (variation), 38
guar gum, 17, 19, 213

H

ham
    Hawaiian Pizza, 53
    Quiche Lorraine (variation), 87
hazelnuts, 213
    Blueberry Hazelnut Crumble
        Coffee Cake, 166
hazelnut flour/meal, 14, 217
    Almond Biscotti (variation),
        142
    Nanaimo Bars, 150
Hearty Beef Stew with Biscuit
    Topping, 62
herbs (fresh), 213
    Basic Rich Biscuits (variation),
        127
    Broccoli and Cheese Soup, 29

Crusty French Baguette
    (variation), 102
Mediterranean Focaccia
    Topping, 106
Pasta Salad, 38
Spaghetti and Meatballs, 56
Stuffing Bread, 98
Hot Cross Buns, 108

I

Irish Soda Bread, 136
iron, 20

L

Lasagna, 58
legumes
    Hearty Beef Stew with Biscuit
        Topping (variation), 62
    Pasta Salad (variation), 38
legume flours, 13–14, 19, 21.
    See also specific types of flour
lemons
    Lemon Meringue Pie, 188
    Lemon Snow with Raspberry
        Coulis, 208
    Lemon Squares, 152
    New York–Style Cheesecake,
        204
    Raspberry Jelly Roll (variation),
        168

M

Mac 'n' Cheese, 54
maple syrup, 213
    Raspberry Pecan Vinaigrette, 41
Mediterranean Focaccia Topping,
    106
Microwave Meatloaf, 61
milk and cream (dairy and
    nondairy), 213
    Almond Pound Cake, 159
    Cheese Soufflé, 60
    Cream Sauce, 91
    Creamy Rice Pudding, 199
    Mac 'n' Cheese, 54
    New England Clam Chowder, 34
    Pumpkin Pie, 189
    Quiche Lorraine, 87
    Red Velvet Frosting, 173
    Scalloped Potatoes, 88
    Seafood Fettuccine, 86
    Toffee Sauce, 203
millet, 10, 21
    Cinnamon Raisin Bread
        (variation), 110

mixers, 209
molasses, 213
    Brown Sandwich Bread, 100
    Ginger Snaps, 144
    Hot Cross Buns, 108
    Mock Date Bran Muffins, 123
    Mock Pumpernickel Loaf, 101
muffins, 120–23
    baking tips, 118
mushrooms
    All-Dressed Pizza, Traditional,
        52
    Cream of Mushroom Soup, 32
    Vegetarian Pizza, 50

N

Nanaimo Bars, 150
New England Clam Chowder,
    34
New York–Style Cheesecake,
    204
noodles. *See* pasta and noodles
nuts, 19, 217. *See also* specific types
    of nuts
    Banana Bread (variation), 124
    Chocolate Chip Cookies
        (variation), 147
    Fruitcake, 164
    Nanaimo Bars, 150
nut flours/meals, 14, 19, 217

O

oats and oat flour, 9, 21
    Apple Crisp, 194
    Date Squares, 151
    Microwave Meatloaf, 61
    Mock Date Bran Muffins, 123
    Oatmeal Raisin Cookies, 143
olive oil, 214
olives, 214
    Mediterranean Focaccia
        Topping, 106
    Pasta Salad, 38
onions
    Cheese Biscuits Two Ways
        (variation), 130
    French Onion Soup, Classic, 33
    Mediterranean Focaccia
        Topping, 106
    Poultry Stuffing, 74
oranges and orange marmalade
    Carrot Raisin Muffins, 122
    Crêpes Suzette, 198
    German Christmas Stollen, 112
Oven-Fried Chicken, 70

P

pancakes and waffles, 44–46
pasta and noodles
    Chicken Noodle Soup, 30
    Lasagna, 58
    Mac 'n' Cheese, 54
    Pasta Salad, 38
    Seafood Fettuccine, 86
    Spaghetti and Meatballs, 56
pastry, 180–82. See also pies and
    tarts
    tips, 178–79
pea flours, 14
Peanut Butter Chunk Cookies,
    148
pecans, 214
    Blueberry Hazelnut Crumble
        Coffee Cake (variation), 166
    Butter Tarts (variation), 186
    Pecan Pie, 190
    Raspberry Pecan Vinaigrette,
        41
pecan flour/meal, 14
    Nanaimo Bars (variation), 150
    Pecan Pastry Two Ways, 182
peel (candied), 214. See also fruit,
    candied
peppers (bell), 211
    All-Dressed Pizza, Traditional,
        52
    Chicken Fingers (variation), 78
    Hawaiian Pizza, 53
    Mediterranean Focaccia
        Topping (variation), 106
    Salmon Patties, 82
    Spaghetti and Meatballs, 56
    Vegetarian Pizza, 50
pies and tarts
    savory, 66, 76, 87
    sweet, 184–90
    tips, 178
pineapple
    Frosted Carrot Cake, 160
    Fruitcake, 164
    Hawaiian Pizza, 53
pizza, 48–53
pork
    Spaghetti and Meatballs, 56
    Tourtière, 66
potatoes
    Chicken Pot Pie, 76
    Fish and Chips, 80
    Hearty Beef Stew with Biscuit
        Topping, 62

    New England Clam Chowder,
        34
    Salmon Patties, 82
    Scalloped Potatoes, 88
potato flour, 16
potato starch, 15, 16, 21
Poultry Stuffing, 74
protein, 20
Pumpkin Pie, 189

Q

Quiche Lorraine, 87
quinoa and quinoa flakes, 10
    Chicken Noodle Soup
        (variation), 30
    Date Squares (variation), 151
quinoa flour, 10, 21
    Brown Sandwich Bread, 100
    Christmas Pudding, 202
    Cinnamon Raisin Bread, 110
    Dinner Rolls, 97
    Focaccia, 104
    Frosted Carrot Cake, 160
    German Christmas Stollen, 112
    Irish Soda Bread, 136
    Mock Pumpernickel Loaf, 101
    Peanut Butter Chunk Cookies,
        148
    Stuffing Bread, 98
    White Bread, 96

R

raisins, 214
    Butter Tarts (variation), 186
    Carrot Raisin Muffins, 122
    Cinnamon Raisin Bread, 110
    Creamy Rice Pudding, 199
    Fruitcake, 164
    German Christmas Stollen, 112
    Hot Cross Buns, 108
    Irish Soda Bread (variation), 136
    Oatmeal Raisin Cookies, 143
raspberries and raspberry jam
    Lemon Snow with Raspberry
        Coulis, 208
    Raspberry Breakfast Danish, 114
    Raspberry Jelly Roll, 168
    Raspberry Pecan Vinaigrette, 41
Red Velvet Cake, 172
Red Velvet Frosting, 173
rice, 10. See also wild rice;
    rice flours (below)
    Chicken Noodle Soup
        (variation), 30
    Creamy Rice Pudding, 199

rice flour, brown, 10, 17, 21
    Almond Pound Cake, 159
    Banana Chocolate Chip
        Muffins, 120
    Basic Rich Biscuits, 127
    Cheese Biscuits Two Ways, 130
    Cinnamon Raisin Bread, 110
    Cornbread, 132
    Cottage Pudding with Brown
        Sugar Sauce, 162
    Crusty French Baguette, 102
    Dinner Rolls, 97
    Frosted Carrot Cake, 160
    German Christmas Stollen, 112
    Irish Soda Bread, 136
    Oatmeal Raisin Cookies
        (variation), 143
    Pastry Two Ways, Classic, 180
    Shortbread Cookies, 146
    Strawberry Shortcake, 128
    Stuffing Bread, 98
    White Bread, 96
rice flour, sweet, 10, 17
    Chicken Fingers, 78
    Veal Parmesan, 64

S

salad dressings, 40–41
salads, 36–38
Salmon Patties, 82
sauces, 90–91, 203
sausage
    All-Dressed Pizza, Traditional,
        52
    Buckwheat Pancakes with
        Mixed Grill, 44
Scalloped Potatoes, 88
seafood. See fish and seafood
seeds, 19. See also flax seeds
Shortbread Cookies, 146
sorghum, 10–12
sorghum flour, 17, 21
    Apple Crisp, 194
    Banana Bread, 124
    Banana Chocolate Chip
        Muffins, 120
    Basic Rich Biscuits, 127
    Blueberry Hazelnut Crumble
        Coffee Cake, 166
    Brown Sandwich Bread, 100
    Buckwheat Pancakes with
        Mixed Grill, 44
    Buttermilk Waffles, Classic, 46
    Carrot Raisin Muffins, 122
    Chocolate Chip Cookies, 147

sorghum flour *(continued)*
　Chocolate Pudding Cake, 200
　Christmas Pudding, 202
　Date Nut Loaf, 126
　Date Squares (variation), 151
　Fruitcake, 164
　German Chocolate Cake, 170
　Ginger Snaps, 144
　Hearty Beef Stew with Biscuit
　　Topping, 62
　Hot Cross Buns, 108
　Mock Date Bran Muffins, 123
　Mock Pumpernickel Loaf, 101
　Pecan Pastry Two Ways, 182
　Red Velvet Cake, 172
　Thin Pizza Crust Two Ways,
　　Classic, 48
　Turkey Gravy (variation), 75
soups, 29–34
　tips, 28
sour cream, 215
　Cheese Biscuits Two Ways, 130
　Frosted Carrot Cake, 160
　New York–Style Cheesecake,
　　204
soy flour, 14, 19, 21
　Fudgy Brownies, 154
Spaghetti and Meatballs, 56
Sponge Cake, 174
starches, 15
　nutrient content, 20–21
　storing, 19
　thickening with, 15–17
Strawberry Shortcake, 128
Stuffing Bread, 98

T

Tacos, 68
Taco Seasoning, 69
tapioca starch (cassava), 1, 16
　Classic Pastry Two Ways, 180

Doughnuts, 206
Pecan Pastry Two Ways, 182
teff flour, 12, 21
　Banana Bread, 124
　Buttermilk Scones, 134
　Buttermilk Waffles, Classic, 46
　Chocolate Pudding Cake, 200
　Crêpes, 196
　Fudgy Brownies, 154
　German Chocolate Cake, 170
　Hot Cross Buns, 108
　Turkey Gravy, 75
thermometers, 22, 210
Toffee Sauce, 203
tomatoes, 215. *See also* tomato
　sauces
　Buckwheat Pancakes with
　　Mixed Grill, 44
　Hearty Beef Stew with Biscuit
　　Topping, 62
　Mediterranean Focaccia
　　Topping, 106
　Pasta Salad, 38
　Spaghetti and Meatballs, 56
　Vegetarian Pizza, 50
tomato sauces
　All-Dressed Pizza, Traditional,
　　52
　Chicken Fingers (variation), 78
　Hawaiian Pizza, 53
　Lasagna, 58
　Microwave Meatloaf, 61
　Triple-Cheese Focaccia
　　Topping, 105
　Veal Parmesan, 64
Tourtière, 66
Traditional All-Dressed Pizza, 52
Triple-Cheese Focaccia Topping,
　105
Turkey, Roast, 72
Turkey Gravy, 75

V

veal
　Spaghetti and Meatballs, 56
　Veal Parmesan, 64
vegetables (mixed). *See also*
　greens; specific vegetables
　Chicken Pot Pie, 76
　Cornbread (variation), 132
　Hearty Beef Stew with Biscuit
　　Topping, 62
　Quiche Lorraine (variation),
　　87
　Vegetarian Pizza, 50

W

walnuts, 215
　Chicken Fingers, 78
　Chocolate Chip Cookies, 147
　Date Nut Loaf, 126
　Frosted Carrot Cake, 160
　Fudgy Brownies, 154
　Irish Soda Bread (variation),
　　136
White Bread, 96
White Cake, 175
wild rice, 21, 215, 287
　Cream of Mushroom Soup
　　(variation), 32
wine and liqueurs
　Crêpes Suzette, 198
　French Onion Soup, Classic
　　(variation), 33
　Seafood Fettuccine, 86

X

xanthan gum, 15, 19

Y

yeast, 17, 19
yogurt, 215
　Strawberry Shortcake, 128

Library and Archives Canada Cataloguing in Publication

Washburn, Donna, author
　100 classic gluten-free comfort food recipes / Donna Washburn & Heather Butt.

Includes index.
ISBN 978-0-7788-0580-9 (softcover)

1. Gluten-free diet — Recipes. 2. Cookbooks. I. Butt, Heather, author II. Title. III. Title: One hundred classic gluten-free comfort food recipes.

RM237.86.W367 2017　　　641.5'639311　　　C2017-903365-4